COMMERCIAL TRUCKS

Donald F. Wood

Motorbooks International
Publishers & Wholesalers ®

To Professor Richard S. Nelson
of San Francisco State University, my long-time
colleague and friend

First published in 1993 by Motorbooks International
Publishers & Wholesalers, PO Box 2, 729 Prospect
Avenue, Osceola, WI 54020 USA

© Donald F. Wood, 1993

Motorbooks International books are also available at
discounts in bulk quantity for industrial or sales-
promotional use. For details write to Special Sales
Manager at the Publisher's address

Library of Congress Cataloging-in-Publication Data
Wood, Donald F.
    Commercial trucks/Donald F. Wood.
       p. cm. — (Motorbooks International
        Crestline series)
    Includes bibliographical references and index.
    ISBN 0-87938-811-0
    1. Trucks—History. I. Title. II. Series: Crestline
    series.
TL230.W654   1993
629.225—dc20   93-30081

On the front cover: A restored 1947 Studebaker stake
bed commercial truck. *Richard Brown*

Printed and bound in the United States of America

Contents

Acknowledgments

Many people helped with this book, including numerous individuals who have assisted the author at other times during the past decade as he has written about old trucks for a number of periodicals. For this particular book, a number of specific individuals also responded to questionnaires I sent to restoration shops or to firms that were actually using old trucks for advertising.

My list of acknowledgments is long: Gary Alexander, San Francisco; American Red Ball World Wide Movers, Indianapolis; Antique Auto Appraisals, Golden, Colorado; Antique Auto Parts Cellar, South Weymouth, Massachusetts; Steven L. Austin, Winross Restorations; Gerald C. Baines, London, Ontario; S. Hatch Barrett, Boise, Idaho; Phill Baumgarten; Clark Beaumont; Ray Borges, Harrah Automobile Foundation; David Brownell, *Special-Interest Autos*; Buffalo Mack, Inc., Buffalo, New York; Don Bunn; Canadian Transport, Ltd., Belleville, Ontario; Tom C. Burke, Central Freight Lines; James D. Carney, National Truck Equipment Association; Carpenter Industries; Central Freight Lines, Inc., Waco, Texas; the late Martha Cedar; Wayne E. Chambers, Jr., Dudreck, DePaul, Ficco & Morgan Advertising; Jim Cherry, The Carpet Coop; Chevs of the '40s, Vancouver, Washington; W.C. Chisholm, Mack Museum; Cliff Churchill, Churchill Truck Lines; Galen Cole, Coles Express; C. Cook Enterprises, Elsmere, Kentucky; Tom Crooks; John J. DeHanes, Masterpiece Miniatures; Robert Dostal, Peter Pan Bus Lines, Inc.; Richard P. Downs, Eady Construction Co.; Eastern Oregon Museum at Haines; Terry Erlich, *Hemmings Motor News*; Everrite Electric Signs, South Milwaukee, Wisconsin; John B. Everitt; Dale Feazell, Hudson Wagon Works; Fatsco Transmission Warehouse, Fairfield, New Jersey; The Filling Station, Sacramento, California; Fisher Auto Transmission, Fairfield, New Jersey; Dennis Fleck, Yellowstone Balloon Adventures; Herbert F. Fleck, Jr., Daley & Wanzer, Inc.; Ron Foerster; R. A. Forslund, Mt. Shasta, California; Roger Fox, Classic Searchlight Service; Fredrickson Motor Express, Charlotte, North Carolina; Bradley S. Gerlach, Valley Baking Co.; Gary F. Gollott, Biloxi, Mississippi; Ken Goudy; Greer Enterprises, Richland, Washington; Greyhound Lines; Eric Hamerstrom; Mark Hamilton, Fort Payne, Alabama; Jerry Hampton, San Francisco State University; William S. Hansen II, A. L. Hansen Mfg. Co.; Joanne & Kent Harkins, Palouse, Washington; Carol A. Harris, W. H. Christie & Sons; Harvey Service, Inc., Wauwatosa, Wisconsin; John L. Hawkins, *Tow Times*; Steven Hobbs, Kokomo, Indiana; Ronald Grantz, Detroit Public Library; Richard Hebert, Rick's Relics; Robert C. Holmes, Holmes Transportation; Ideal Truck Lines, Inc., Norton, Kansas; Industrial Steel Products, Buffalo, New York; Dave Inglis, Dave's Automotive Machine; Zoe James; Bob Jasper, Jasper Custom Auto Upholstery; Rolland Jerry; John's Truck Parts, Wurtsboro, New York; Philip B. Johnson, Forest Service, U.S.D.A.; C. A. Jones, Jr., Nashville, Georgia; Clive T. Jones, Edmonton, Alberta; Mark Keilen, Keilen's Auto Restoring; Karl K. Kordoban, Lake Milton, Ohio; Ron Kramp, Elk Lake, Ontario; Kron's Meat Shoppe, Woodland, Maryland; Ron LaMacchia,

Louisville Cabinet Co.; LeBaron Bonney Co.; Harold E. Layman, Volvo White, Dublin, Virginia; Greg Lennes, International Harvester; Frank J. Lichtanski, Monterey-Salinas Transit; Dennis Lucas, Wood Affair; Jerry D. Lundberg, Sterling Transit; Mack Products, Moberly, Missouri; McClain Leasing & Sales, Anderson, Indiana; Spike Michaud, Michaud Bus Lines; Midstate Sign Company, Murfreesboro, Tennessee; Midwest Emery Freight System, McCook, Illinois; National Truck School, San Rafael, California; James L. Nelson, Atlanta; Richard S. Nelson, San Francisco State University; David Norton; Alex Nunez, National Spring Co.; Obsolete Ford Parts, Inc., Oklahoma City; Oklahoma City Freightliner, Oklahoma City, Oklahoma; Old Chev Trucks, Pasadena, Texas; Older Car Parts, Seattle, Washington; Olivine Corporation, Bellingham, Washington; Gene Olson; Mike Pagel; Dan Pritchett; Clayton M. Press, Sr.; Bert Prouty; Michael Querio, Royal Trucking; Bart Rawson; Rechtien International Trucks, Miami, Florida; Ward Reiss, Oakpark, Virginia; Joy Rich, The Salvation Army Archives; Edward M. Rider, Procter & Gamble; Risberg's Truck Lines, Portland, Oregon; Tim Sabath, Goodyear; Robert F. Saeman, Cross Plains, Wisconsin; Steve Sass, A.N.D. Service; Peter Scalamandre, Freeport, New York; Schaeffer & Long, Inc., Magnolia, New Jersey; Christian Schmidt Brewing Co., Philadelphia; Fred Schweser, Bird Automotive; J. A. Schwind, Beverage Distributors, Inc.; Scritch's Auto Restoration, Glendale, California; Mark A. Segale, Tukwila, Washington; Vern R. Sell, Heavy Chevy Truck Parts; Tom Shelton, Franklin, Tennessee; Jon Skul, The Ertl Co.; W. E. Smith, Sherwin-Williams; Marv Silverstein, New Era Toys; Smith Transportation Co., Santa Maria, California; Daniel J. Solomon, E & J Gallo Winery; Wayne Sorensen; Jerry Spencer, U & ME Moving and Storage; George Sperl, Johnson Controls; Lynn Steele, Denver, North Carolina; John Stevens, *TRUCKS* Magazine; Roy E. Strevel, Jr., Spring Lake, Michigan; Grover Swank; Roy Stewart; Tod Swormstedt, ST Publications; Tazewell Towing, Pekin, Illinois; Jack Tenge, San Francisco State University; Dan Triggs, Blue Bird Body Co.; Robert S. Truesdale, Gulf Oil Products; C. M. Turley, Riverside, California; Robert Turnquist, Hibernia Auto Restorations; Lloyd Van Horn; David Vermilion, The Dawes Arboretum; Donna & Howard Vigen; George H. von Paris, Timonium, Maryland; Greg Ward, Urbana, Ohio; Bill West; Ed Whittington; Wisconsin Culvert Co.; Wise Ford, Hazlehurst, Mississippi; Doreen J. Wood; James A. Wren, Motor Vehicle Manufacturers Association; and WW Motor Cars & Parts, Broadway, Virginia.

Donald F. Wood
San Francisco State University
January 1993

Introduction

Americans have long been interested in the history of transportation, possibly because of the industry's importance to our country and the fact that transportation threads run richly through the tapestries of our social and economic well-being.

As we celebrate the 100th anniversary of the automobile and truck, it is appropriate to ask about the people and machines that have had such a profound impact on our highway transportation system. Trucks and autos are closely related in technology, in their sharing of roadways, and sharing of user taxes. Both did—and are doing—much to shape our country, our patterns of living, and our lifestyles.

We will focus on a smaller part of the big picture and look at the restored trucks that many businesses use as advertising tools. Businesses use restored trucks for advertising for several reasons, not the least of which is the owner's personal interest in trucks. An equally important reason is the public's recognition that trucks and trucking made an important contribution to the development of each individual community and to the nation as a whole. Someone viewing an old truck recognizes that he or she is seeing a vehicle that, when working, made a contribution to our nation's economic development and well-being.

A note of apology should be given to purists when it comes to identification of truck model years and authenticity of various truck and body features. Truck model years were never identi-fied as precisely as they were for automobiles; and truck owners have always had a more care-free attitude about making additions or changes to a truck and its body. (Some of the individuals we contacted regarding old trucks they owned and restored had to guess at the year of manufacture themselves.)

This book is divided into two parts. The first (chapters 1 through 7) is introductory and historical and provides many examples and pictures of old trucks and the advertising functions they initially performed. Pictures are provided to give ideas to potential restorers.

The second part (chapters 8 through 12) deals with the present-day selection and restoration of old trucks and their use for advertising purposes. Insofar as we know, all the trucks mentioned in this section are being—or have been—used for advertising. Sometimes, technically, they have not been restored but, more correctly, maintained in their original condition. The degree to which each is used for advertising purposes varies.

In a few instances, old trucks with a firm's name painted on the side were photographed at truck shows, and we assumed this to be an advertising activity. Occasionally we were unable to trace the names of firms painted on a truck's sides. They may have been made up, or they may have been the names of predecessors to today's firms that existed when the trucks were new.

Chapter 1

The Advertising Function

Advertising, a part of the marketing function, involves an attempt to reach a large audience with a positive message concerning a firm's product or service. It can take several forms, and the advertising message is repeated over and over.

This book deals with only one form of advertising: the use of trucks to draw attention to a firm. Those who use old trucks for advertising purposes feel that their target audience may have either a specific interest in old vehicles or a more general interest in historical items. They hope that the old truck will attract people's attention to the extent that they look at the truck and read or see whatever message is associated with it.

The use of an old truck for advertising is especially appropriate for firms that have been in business for some time and want to convey a sense of stability. (They might try to buy and restore a truck dating to the year their firm was founded.) It's also appropriate for firms already associated with trucking: motor carriers, truck dealers, or firms that use large delivery fleets. Some firms have adopted an old truck as their advertising symbol.

Old trucks have been and can be used for advertising in a number of ways, which will be detailed in subsequent chapters. The most common use over the years is in local parades. Some of the old pictures accompanying this chapter show trucks carrying either product displays or a public-spirited float.

In addition to exposing an advertising message to a large number of viewers, a restored old truck participating in a parade is considered a contribution to the community and a public relations gesture. (Public relations is not the same as advertising; it's associated more with creating and maintaining a reservoir of community "good will.") Many of the advertising tasks performed by restored old trucks are probably of a public relations nature. Some firms have even donated restored trucks to local museums that display items associated with their area's history.

Restored old trucks are also often used for advertising in trade shows, especially those associated with automotive products. Old trucks are "gimmicks" or "hooks" that will attract people and are still sufficiently unique that they stand out and are difficult for competitors to match quickly.

Restoring trucks also brings tax advantages to their owners because advertising can be counted as a legitimate business expense. No doubt some old car buffs who happen to own a business may have decided to restore old trucks instead and charge the costs against their firm. If you're interested in restoring an old truck and using it to advertise your business, make sure you analyze the effectiveness of the old truck idea in terms of reaching prospective customers.

You will find in this book a few mentions and pictures of old automobiles used for advertising. These examples are harder to find, probably for tax reasons and because a truck is more likely to be closely related to business or commercial uses. Also, it's more acceptable, feasible, and effective to paint large advertising signs and pictures on a truck than on an automobile.

Austin, 1930

Snowshoe's Advertising Service drivers of Reno, Nevada, drove this 1930 Austin to Los Angeles for promotion. It appears that the overhead signs were mounted on a hinged frame that could be dismantled so it would lay flat for highway travel. *The Whittington Collection, California State University, Long Beach*

For what it's worth, it is widely believed that messages on new trucks are effective advertising. (A few old pictures in this book are of trucks that did nothing but carry ads.) An article entitled "Trucks Carry More Than Freight" in the June 1985 issue of *The Private Carrier* started out: "Recent studies have shown that advertising on trucks is one of the most effective and least expensive ways to advertise, provided that the truck graphics are produced by a competent fleet graphics converter.

"After several progressive companies pioneered the use of trucks as moving billboards, many other companies began to follow suit, and advertising on trucks is growing rapidly. Trucks are now seen in increasing numbers displaying bold, spectacular graphics, advertising goods and services for numerous companies. Many of these graphics messages are enhanced by large pictorials, produced with four-color process screen printing on pressure-sensitive decal materials."

The article also made reference to a study conducted by the American Trucking Associa-tions with respect to the reactions of people viewing fleet graphics:

- 67 percent favored fleet graphics
- 91 percent notice words and pictures
- 35 percent look more closely, and ·
- 29 percent make a buying decision based on their impression of the company vehicle.

While use of new trucks on the highway cannot be equated with the use of a restored old truck in a parade or at a trade show, there are some parallels. An important one is the fact that the truck and its appearance reflect upon the owning firm.

While trucks were—and are—built to move from point A to point B and much of this book is written on this premise, we would be remiss if we failed to acknowledge that a very important advertising role of trucks is performed while they are parked. Trucks can be substituted for signs or billboards that are otherwise prohibited by zoning or other restrictions. Thus, it is not unusual to see a truck parked every weekend and evening in a very conspicuous spot where it,

Packard, circa 1917
A Packard truck with a patriotic float during the World War I era. *Reading Body Works*

Reo Speedwagon, circa 1920s
A machine shop in Marysville, California, decorated this early 1920s Reo Speedwagon for a parade and a little promotion. *California State Library*

and the advertising message it carries on its side, can be seen by those passing. Trucks used for this purpose are often not old, they might simply be any or all that are in the owner's fleet. When valuable old trucks are used, their owners should be concerned about vandalism.

You will find pictures of both routine trucks as well as some very unique rigs that were used by businesses as they promoted and delivered their products.

Mack Bulldog, 1928
The Baldwin Locomotive Works had an apparent preference for Republicans. Baldwin's promotional truck was a Mack Bulldog. *H.L. Broadbelt*

Mack, 1929
The Keystone Sand & Supply Company displayed a keystone figure consisting of small pebbles on a load of sand.

Chevrolet, 1942
A 1942 Chevrolet carrying a group of E. R. Squibb & Sons employees in a parade. *E. R. Squibb & Sons*

Ford Model T, circa 1915
A Ford Model T automobile used as a commercial vehicle for a photographer. Across the windshield ran the lettering "Charles J. Herbert, Photographer, Traverse City." *Harrah's Automobile Collection, Reno*

Unknown make, circa 1920s
A building company carried this half-sized home as a parade display. *Motor Vehicle Manufacturers Association*

International, circa mid-1930s
The Washington Egg & Poultry Cooperative Association carried a high school band in a parade. Today's insurance policies would not allow a truck to carry such a large group. *Navistar Archives*

Buggy and 1933 Ford, 1940
A 1940 picture, taken just before a parade in Emporia, Kansas. At the left was a horse-drawn buggy (pulled by an automobile) carrying people dressed in 1870s costumes. To the right was a 1933 Ford with a display showing library workers in contemporary dress. *Lyon County, Kansas, Historical Museum*

Spare tire advertising, circa 1930s
Up until the mid-1930s, most automobile spare tires were mounted outside the automobile, either at the rear or in the front fender wells, as shown here. Spare-tire covers that carried an advertising message were widely promoted. *Motor Vehicle Manufacturers Association*

Oldsmobile, 1935
Brown and Williamson Tobacco Company used this rig to promote Kool Cigarettes. It's believed that the vehicle was used to distribute free sample packs at fairs, baseball games, and so on. It was carried on a 1935 Oldsmobile "commercial" chassis. "Commercial" chassis were provided by many auto builders and consisted of the chassis and front body back to about the driver's area. Individual body builders then would add an ambulance, limousine, or other unique body to complete the unit. *National Automotive History Collection, Detroit Public Library*

Kelly, circa 1920s
Special displays were placed on trucks and used to promote moving pictures in the early days of Hollywood. Here a Kelly truck was promoting the movie *The Great Air Robbery. Oregon Historical Society*

Sterling, 1920
This 1920 vintage Sterling was used to promote the movie *The Lost World. Western Reserve*

Chevrolet, 1937
This 1937 Chevrolet pulled a trailer with a caged Chinese Buffalo, which was appearing in the MGM movie *The Good Earth. Baker Library, Harvard University*

Traveling billboard, circa 1920s
"Trucks are traveling billboards" is a phrase that is often used. There was a time when advertising space was sold on the sides of vehicles. This rig carried ads for a smoke shop, a jeweler, a bank, an auto paint shop, a hat blocker and cleaner, a bakery, a hardware store, and Mrs. A. N. Munn, whose specialty was "pleating, hemstitching, and fancy buttons." *Texas State Library*

Cart before the horse, circa 1920s
This rig advertised three different businesses, which may have been a play on the words "cart before the horse." *Weber's, Fort Worth*

Ford, 1935
Trucks were also important to the advertising industry. Here was a 1935 Ford used by Foster and Kleiser to service a billboard. *Foster and Kleiser.*

International, 1939
A 1939 International used by an oil company to service neon signs at its service stations. *Navistar Archives*

Step-van, circa 1990s
On the roof of this step-van was a hay bale, milk cans, and a large egg. The truck was spotted on a street near a shopping center in Costa Mesa, California.

Chevrolet El Camino, 1959
This 1959 Chevrolet El Camino was parked in front of a muffler shop and filled with old mufflers and tailpipes in Ogden, Utah.

Volkswagen, circa 1980s
A VW van advertising a heating and plumbing service. It was being pushed by a tin-man figure.

Ford, 1948
This 1948 Ford pickup was permanently mounted on concrete—half art, half promotion.

Double-decker bus, circa 1980s
An old London double-decker bus advertising a roadside tourist attraction.

"Toe Truck," circa 1980s
This "Toe Truck" was spotted on the roof of a Seattle, Washington, towing firm. The personalized license plate read "MR TOE."

Chapter 2

Traveling Billboards

Before the days of trucks, merchants painted their wagons in bright colors and decorated them gaily with lettering, stripes, and even pictures. This practice carried over to motor trucks. The merchants realized that the trucks' sides had potential for carrying an advertising message.

This is the first of several chapters that consist almost entirely of pictures of old trucks to illustrate the wide range of trucks and the

Studebaker, 1938
This top-of-the line 1938 Studebaker was christened by a beauty queen with a bottle of champagne. This

Studebaker Special, nicknamed *Miss America*, delivered for Paul's Kreamo bread. *Richard Quinn*

Unknown make, circa 1910s
The make of truck is unknown, and the original negative is deteriorating. However, note the picture of the phonograph and the elaborate lettering. Note also the sign above the windshield. The picture was taken in London, Ontario. *Public Archives of Canada*

numerous ways they were painted, decorated, or otherwise modified to make them more effective agents for advertising and promotion. Another function of this chapter of the book is to give the potential restorer some ideas of how to decorate a restored rig in a relatively authentic manner.

This chapter contains pictures of conventional truck bodies and styles, where the decoration was provided by a sign painter, a striper, or a decal applicator.

Because these old pictures are all in black and white, we are usually forced to guess what the original truck colors were. Also, we must often guess at the process used to create and apply the graphics to the truck although earlier in the century, labor was relatively cheap and some of the processes—especially the individually executed pictures—must have involved a large number of hours of an artist's labor.

While the trucks and truck body styles shown in this chapter are typical, they were somewhat more extensively painted in order to promote a product or service. Where the decoration or design appears unique, a comment will be made.

International, circa 1910
Pictured in front of the Betsy Ross house was a high-wheeled International, circa 1910, with a large picture of the battleship Pennsylvania. *Navistar Archives*

White, circa 1910s
An early White, painted white and fitted with a fabric roof. It was used by Beeman's Pepsin Gum. *Volvo/White*

White, 1910
The portrait on the side of this 1910 White laundry truck used in Portland, Oregon, showed the owner's plant or factory. This was a common theme of many pictures painted on the sides of early trucks. Shown in this plant scene were trucks similar to the one pictured here. Barely visible were similar light panels on the sides, containing miniatures of the picture we're seeing. *Volvo/White*

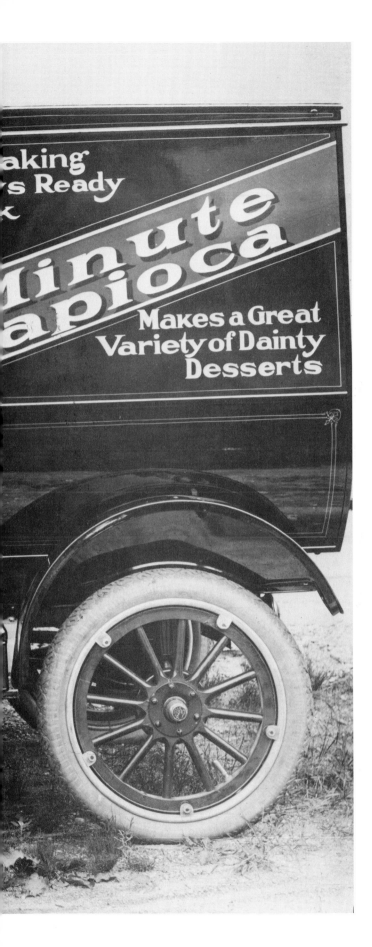

Ford Model T, circa 1915
This circa 1915 Ford Model T was driven by a Minute Tapioca salesman in San Francisco. Photo was taken in 1919. *General Foods*

Mack, circa 1915
An early Mack, used by a candy company in New York City. Note the details of the leaf design. *Mack Museum*

Ford Model T, circa 1915
This drug store's Ford Model T had advertising slogans painted on both wheels. *Harrah's Automobile Collection, Reno*

23

Ford, circa 1915

The trailer on this baker's rig was originally horse-drawn; a fifth wheel was added to the Ford coupe that was substituted for the horse. Nine different styles of lettering were used on the wagon's side, and it looked like a sampler demonstrating the range of the sign painter's lettering abilities. *Fruehauf*

Kalamazoo, circa 1915

A Kalamazoo truck, a somewhat obscure make built in the years 1913–1920 in the Michigan city with the same name. This 3 1/2 ton Kalamazoo dump truck was used by The Upjohn Company. Note the pinstriping. *The Upjohn Company*

International, circa 1917
An early truck-trailer rig used by the Scott-Powell dairy—its Golden A Guernsey Milk was advertised as "Fresher by a Day." The tractor was a World War I-vintage International. Note the contrasting dark and light colors. *Pullman Trailmobile*

Ford Model T fleet, circa 1915
A row of Ford Model Ts used to deliver "Hubig's Famous Honey-Fruit Pies." The tires have holes drilled through the sides to provide a more cushioned ride. *O. V. Hunt Collection, Birmingham Public Library*

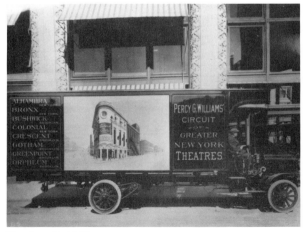

Packard, 1911
This 1911 Packard was used to carry stage sets between a chain of theaters. One of the theaters, the Bushwick, in Brooklyn, New York, was pictured. *Motor Vehicle Manufacturers Association*

International, circa 1915
A lion, a fitting symbol for the Monarch Laundry, was displayed on the side of this International. *Navistar Archives*

Pierce-Arrow, circa 1915
This brick company used a brick pattern painted on the side of its Pierce-Arrow truck. *Library, University of Michigan*

Ford Model T, circa 1915
A sign painter's truck, a Ford Model T. Top hood panel was painted white and contained the slogan: "Signs better than the rest." *Library of Congress*

Ford Model T, circa 1915
A snuff salesman used this Ford Model T with a small, enclosed truck body in place of the auto's original rear seat. *US Tobacco Museum*

Pierce-Arrow, circa 1915
This Pierce-Arrow was unloaded from the side. The several doors, bracing, and hardware did not make the sign painter's job easy. *Press Tank Co.*

GMC, circa 1920
A Cincinnati trucking firm used this GMC from about 1920. Note that the firm's route structure was pictured on a panel attached to the stake sides. Early trucking firms often painted their route maps on their trucks. *Pullman Trailmobile*

Mack, circa 1920
Fancy lettering on a light-colored Mack tank truck from about 1920. As the sign writing on the tank stated, the tank carried Polarine oil. *Mack Museum*

Moreland, circa 1920
Side views of a Moreland moving van from about 1920. *University of California, Los Angeles Library*

Mack, circa 1920s
Trucks with heavy bumpers often had signs painted on front. This was a Mack, probably carrying a cement mixer. *Mack Museum*

Mack, circa 1920s
A Mack tractor-trailer used by a dairy. The Dodds Alternative Dairy company's motto, "Quality Tells," could just have well been the motto of Mack. *Fruehauf*

Moreland, circa 1920
Front views of the Moreland moving van. *University of California, Los Angeles Library*

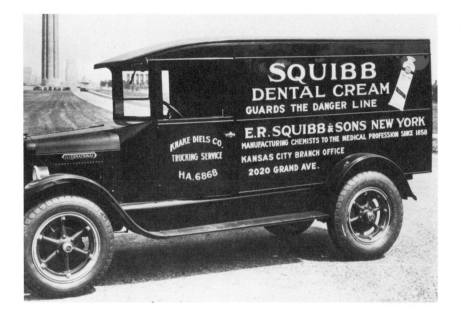

International, circa 1925
This mid-1920s International was used by the Kansas City branch office of E. R. Squibb & Sons. *E.R. Squibb & Sons*

GMC, circa 1925
A GMC tow truck from the mid-1920s. Barely visible was the hood ornament, shaped like an automobile. *Silent Hoist & Crane Co.*

Gersix, circa 1925
A Gersix truck built in Seattle and a predecessor to the Kenworth, lavishly decorated to advertise Rainier Oil Company's gasoline. As the signwriting stated, the gasoline provided "mountains of Power." *Paccar*

Mack, circa 1920s
A Mack tractor trailer used by Kroger with plain but
attractive lettering. *Fruehauf*

Dodge, circa 1925
This photo, taken in Buffalo, New York, showed a C-
cab Dodge from the mid-1920s. *General Mills, Inc.,
Archives*

Dodge, circa 1925
This neatly done Dodge had "top-of-the-line" trim, including whitewalls. As the door signwriting stated, this was an "Advertising Car," and showed its advertising license number. *Wm. J. Wrigley, Jr. Co.*

Dodge, circa 1925
There's a variation in quality of decorations on this Dodge truck. The word "EASY" looks as though it was done with a fairly crude stencil. However, on the cab door is a detailed picture of a small electric motor. *Freeborn County Historical Society, Albert Lea, Minnesota*

Ford Model A, circa 1925
This Ford Model A pickup had a canopied body, with a flat sign attached on both sides. Note advertising on spare tire cover. *Western Michigan University Archives, Budford Green Collection*

Dodge, 1926
This 1926 Dodge was used by a sampling crew, help-
ing to promote Camay Soap. *Proctor & Gamble*

GMC, 1927
A snappy-looking 1927 GMC panel used by a meat distributor, Associated Meat Company. *Blackhawk Classic Auto Collection*

Mack Bulldog, 1929
The lettering had to be spaced around the wooden framework on this trailer. Barely visible at lower front of trailer are words: "J.C. Fisel, builder." Tractor is a Mack Bulldog; the picture was taken in 1929. *Mack Trucks, Inc.*

Mack BJ, 1929
A 1929 Mack BJ with the mover's "No Kick" slogan
incorporated into the artwork. *Mack Trucks*

Ford Model AA, 1930
This 1930 photo shows a Ford Model AA tractor. The
tractor's chassis was 12ft, 9in long with a 14ft, 3in
body. Tires were solid at 36x6. The trailer's side is
completely devoted to advertisement for Monarch cat-
sup. *Pullman Trailmobile*

Ford Model A, circa 1925
A Ford Model A used by Hellmann to promote the firm's mayonnaise. *Charles Wacker Company*

International, circa 1930s
An early 1930s C-cab International truck advertising Weber's Pullman bread. *Navistar Archives*

International, circa 1930s
Detail of the C-cab International bread truck. The signboard on the running board holds a poster promoting "magic cards" wrapped in the bread. *Navistar Archives*

Mack, circa 1930s
A Mack delivery truck, from the early 1930s, used by Land O'Lakes butter for advertising and delivery. *Mack Museum*

Chevrolet, circa 1930
A Chevrolet coupe from about 1930 fitted with a box used by a worker who serviced milking machines. *Duke D'Ambra, Watkins Community Museum*

Federal, circa 1930
A 1930-1931 Federal tank truck, with the body painted a different color than the cab, hood, and fenders. *The Heil Co.*

Indiana, 1932
Loading up wares into a 1932 Indiana truck, which must have been painted a multitude of colors. Note the bus-like signboard above the windshield; whether it displayed more than one sign is unknown. *Volvo/White*

Dodge, 1934
Ben-Hur in his chariot was featured on the side of the 1934 Dodge panel used by Ben-Hur Original Drip Coffee. *Eight-Point Trailer Corp., Los Angeles*

White, 1934
Note the fancy checked pattern painted on the sides of this 1934 White Model 702 step-van, which sported a drop frame. The truck was used for advertising and delivering Kraft's Miracle Whip Salad Dressing—as the signwriting stated, it was "Kitchen Fresh." *Volvo/White*

Dodge, 1934
A 1934 Dodge used by Rieck's Dairy with a body built by Mayer Body Corporation of Pittsburgh, Pennsylvania. *Mayer Body Corp.*

GMC, circa 1930s
This late 1930s GMC cab-over-engine stake was covered by a large tarp with lettering and logo painted on the canvas. The trucks carried a General Electric traveling exhibit of modern switchgear. *General Electric*

Dart, 1934
A Dart truck, a make that is still being manufactured in Kansas City, Missouri. The truck and trailer bodies were manufactured by Soldner of Salina. Placard racks at the curved front of both the truck box and trailer box hold replaceable signs. *Kansas State Historical Society, Topeka*

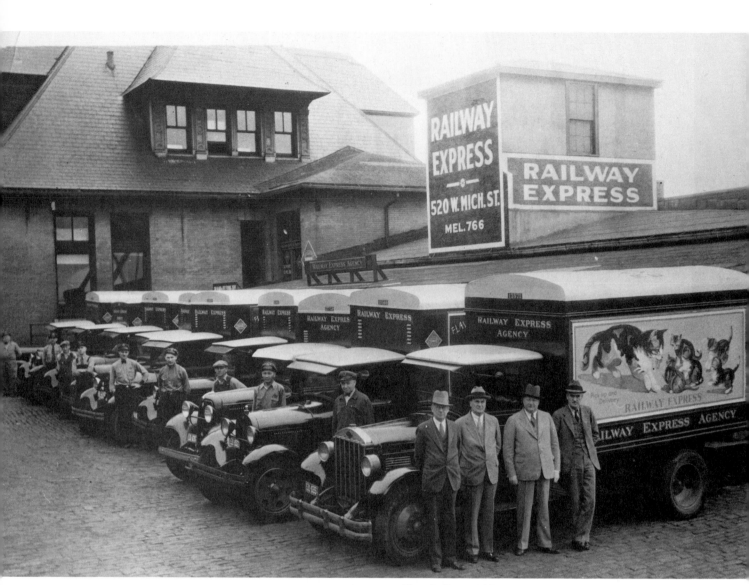

Truck fleet, 1935

The Railway Express Agency was owned by the nation's railroads and provided intercity rail service for small parcels using special cars on passenger trains. Fleets of trucks such as this one, pictured in Duluth, Minnesota, in 1935, provided local pickups and deliveries. The posters held in the side signboards were changed from time to time. They were probably pasted on, similar to billboards. (Wrinkles are visible in the picture of the cats.) *Northeast Minnesota Historical Center*

Ford, 1935

A 1935 Ford, used in Texas. The emblem on the front curved corner of the cab showed a railroad steam engine and a ship, stating: "Houston—where eighteen railroads meet the sea." The small lettering in front of the cab says "R. R. COM PERMIT 12439," with the first letters standing for Texas Railroad Commission, which also regulated motor carriers. Trucks used by carriers needed permit numbers painted on them, and in many states the truck's taxable weight had to be painted on in small letters and numbers. *Pullman Trailmobile*

Autocar, 1935
A trailer finished with a burnished metal. The tractor is a 1935 Autocar Model UNT with a 109in wheelbase. The trailer was a Fruehauf unit measuring 80in high, 27ft long, and 89in wide. The truck was used to carry pies from Chicago to Milwaukee for Mrs. Wagner's Pies company. Trailer capacity was 6,000 pies. *American Institute of Baking*

Ford, circa 1935
A refrigerated Ford truck used to haul Pfeifer's Flavor Fresh Sausage. *A.L. Hansen Mfg. Co.*

Ford, circa 1935
Body hardware on the refrigerated Pfeifer's Flavor Fresh Sausage Ford truck. *A.L. Hansen Mfg. Co.*

Ford fleet, 1936
These 1936 Fords had Disney characters on the sides to advertise Mickey Mouse Cakes. As the signwriting stated, "No foolin'—they're good." Note that the rear truck has sound equipment. The trucks were Model 112 panel deliveries powered by Ford's V-8 engine. *Ford Archives*

Studebaker, 1936
A 1936 Studebaker tractor with a
classic style of lettering on the cab
doors pulling a beautiful streamlined trailer with modern-style lettering. *Gillig Corp.*

A message to be heeded, 1938
Sign on the rear of a Texan baker's
truck. *Texas Department of Transportation*

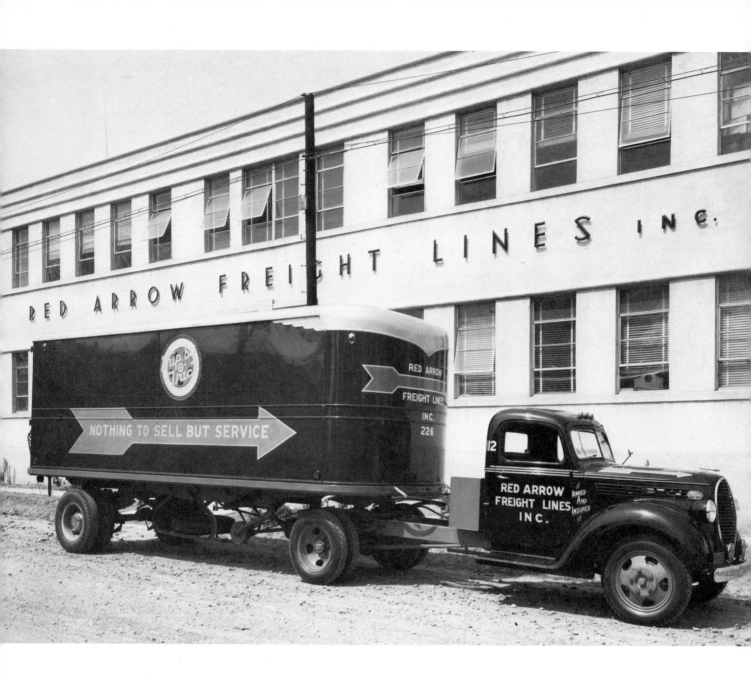

Ford, 1938
A 1938 Ford with arrow patterns on the sides and front of the trailer and on top of the truck's hood. Emblem on the Fruehauf trailer shows a tire and says, "Ship by truck." Similar emblems were used at various times throughout the country. *Fruehauf*

White, circa 1930s
A Richmond moving company pictured a historical attraction above the phrase "Visit our historical city, Richmond, VA." The truck was a White, nicknamed *The Belle*. *Volvo/White*

Mack, circa 1930s
A late 1930s Mack sleeper cab, with a tarpaulin cover-ing the open trailer. The white sidewall tires were unusual. *Galveston Truck Lines*

International, circa 1937
An International from the late 1930s with plain letter-ing and an attractive image showing a worker at a forge. Bodywork was by Mayer. *Mayer Body Corp.*

International, circa 1940
Purina's checkerboard pattern was painted across this Fruehauf trailer in dramatic styling. The tractor was an International from about 1940. *Fruehauf*

Mack, circa 1940
A tranquil scene painted on side of the Wilton Farm Dairy's Mack. *Motor Vehicle Manufacturers Association*

Mack, circa 1940
The Scheffler System, a motor carrier, donated trailer-side space to a local minor-league baseball team, the Sheboygan Indians. Truck was a Mack. *Pullman Trailmobile*

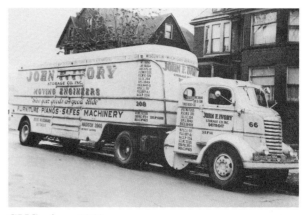

GMC, circa 1940s
Note the incredible number of state operating authority numbers on this interstate moving van—advertisements in themselves showing the company's wide business range! The tractor was a 1940s GMC. *W.A. Drew*

Dodge, 1940
"Like sleeping on a cloud" was the advertising phrase for the Fort Pitt Bedding Company and its Sealy Mattress line. The truck was a 1940 Dodge with a body built by Mayer. Note the covered rear wheelwells and their streamlined logo. *Mayer Body Corp.*

Ford, 1941
A 1941 Ford cab-over with a route map painted on the
side of the Mayer-built body. *Mayer Body Corp.*

Chevrolet, 1941
This 1941 Chevrolet tank truck picked up milk from
farmers for the Challenge Dairy. *Challenge Dairy*

Ford, 1942
Plain signs advertising Bond Bread on the sides of this
chromeless, wartime 1942 Ford. The body was by
McCabe-Powers Auto Body Company of St. Louis, Missouri. *McCabe Powers*

White, 1943
A 1943 White Model S-116-A step-van used by a direct mail advertising firm named Ahrend. The small figures along the side show analysis, merchandising plan, copy, art, execution, addressing, and mailing. The panel at rear stated, "Memo: Call Ahrend for everything in Direct Mail." *Volvo/White*

White, circa 1940s
An early 1940s White cab-over-engine used by Bekins Van Lines. Note the sleeper cab and extendable turn signal arm. *The Bekins Co.*

Dodge, circa 1940s
A patriotic message to Buy War Bonds was painted on side of this 1940s Dodge. *Eight-Point Trailer Corp., Los Angeles*

Diamond-T, circa 1940s
A Diamond-T pulling a semi-trailer carrying a billboard-size advertisement for the Wiarton, Canada, recreational area. *Ontario Trucking Association*

Chevrolet, circa 1940s
Contented hogs were pictured on this late 1940s Chevrolet that carried Prom-Min Feeds hog supplements. *Omaha Body & Equipment Co.*

International, circa 1940s
Signs that could be read from above were used for trucks with routes near apartment buildings. (Today they're used to make it easier to spot hijacked trailers.) Truck was a 1940s International in the service of Minnehaha Cleaners of Minneapolis-St. Paul. *Navistar Archives*

Kenworth fleet, circa 1947
Braswell Motor Freight Lines had a "B" built into in its grille guards. Trucks were postwar Kenworths. *Paccar*

Chevrolet, 1951
A 1951 Chevrolet moving van, nicknamed *The Gypsy*.
The Gerstenslager Co.

Diamond-T, circa 1950s
A refuse body on a late 1950s Diamond-T operated by
B. Manzo & Son of New York state. *Mort Glasofer*

White, circa 1950s
An early 1950s White coal dump body. Body trimmers referred to this body side as a "picture frame" style since it was free of obstructions and could accommodate any lettering or design. *Press Tank Co.*

Ford, 1960
An unrestored 1960 Ford with a moving body provides plenty of space for a sign.

Chapter 3

The Third Dimension: Adding Catchy Shapes

This chapter shows examples of three-dimensional figures or embellishments that were sometimes used on trucks to advertise a product or service. Most of these date from the period before there was much concern with wind resistance. A related problem was caused by attaching rivets to the body—over time the twisting of the truck would result in enlarged rivet holes through which rain water would leak.

The pictures should give potential truck restorers some ideas as to how you might use figures, raised lettering, or other three-dimensional devices to give some added advertising value to the truck you choose to restore. You will have to use care when attempting to use some of the embellishments illustrated here; they add to the truck's exterior dimensions, add wind resistance—even if the restored rig is on an open trailer—and may be targets of vandals and thieves.

"Streamlining" is a term associated with the changes that took place in automobile styling during the 1930s. Individuals familiar with autos of that era know that in 1930 all autos had flat, boxy shapes, while by 1940, all autos were much lower, had few flat shapes, and appeared to offer much less wind resistance. Streamlining was considered by some as an aspect of the Art Deco movement that also influenced architecture and furniture designs during the period between the two world wars.

Trucks were not streamlined as much as autos for several reasons. One relates to costs and economics of mass production: trucks were much less numerous than autos. Lowering of

Hewitt, circa 1905
A one-ton Hewitt built just after the turn of the century. Note the large roof-mounted placard on both sides of the truck advertising the Monarch Bulldog Paint & Varnish Remover. *Smithsonian Institution*

Ford Model TT, circa 1920
A wooden cutout of a "Sierra Club Ginger Ale" bottle was mounted on the side of this stake truck, a Model TT Ford from about 1920. *FABCO*

vehicle's roof lines cut into usable carrying space, and any additions of shaped sheet metal was at the expense of the truck's weight-carrying and/or cubic capacity. Nonetheless, trucks were streamlined in several ways.

Ford Model T, circa 1920
This Ford Model T used by a Los Angeles auto dealer had wheel figures on the sides of the cab. *Crown Coach*

• Truck chassis and cab manufacturers built more stylish fronts, with V-shaped radiator grilles, sloping windows, and so on.
• Mass production body builders also added minor touches to the body styles they marketed. For example, in looking at literature for Heil petroleum tank bodies during the thirties, one can see the top-of-the-line streamlined bodies that blend easily with the truck cab's roof and side lines, the rear wheel covers are tear-shaped, and some even have fender skirts.
• Individual body builders turned out custom (virtually one-of-a-kind) rigs for some customers.

The advertising advantages of using a streamlined tank body can be seen in this quotation from the Heil literature: "Trim, attractive Heil Quality Built streamline truck tanks are doing a real selling job for oil marketers who are so strongly convinced of the attention value of fine looking truck tank equipment that they willingly make the extra investment which streamline design requires.

"Think of it! A truck tank covers 80 to 100 miles daily parading the oil marketer's name and tradebrands before the eyes of thousands

Mack, circa 1920s
Coca-Cola cutouts along the truck and trailer body of this bottler's rig. Truck was a Mack from the 1920s. *Coca-Cola*

of...prospective customers. Heil streamline design makes favorable and lasting impressions. No form of advertising is as cheap as the day-in and day-out reminder advertising value built into Heil...streamline truck tanks. Realizing this fact, many oil marketers charge the extra cost of Heil streamline design to advertising expense."

To individuals interested in the history of trucking, the most famous streamlined trucks were those of the Canadian brewers during the 1930s. Prevented from many forms of advertising, the brewers developed extremely streamlined truck-trailer units to promote their beers and ales. Best-known of the trucks were those designed by Count Alexis de Sakhnoffsky for Labatt Brewers. The trucks were "painted a brilliant Labatt red," and a single truck "required twenty-seven books of gold leaf for lettering." One Labatt's rig was restored (or replicated) in 1984.

If you are considering restoring a streamlined truck, remember that because the originals were often produced in single or small numbers, many parts and pieces will have to be hand-crafted, and restoration will be very time-consuming. However, when your job is complete, you will have a truly unique truck.

Ford Model T, circa 1920s
This Model T Ford from the late 1920s had a roof sign running the length of the body. It was part of the curved racks for holding rolled-up carpets. *McCabe Powers*

Ford Model A, circa 1928
On top of the cab of the left truck, a Ford Model A, stood the figure of a polar bear. The firm's name was "Theo. Poehler Mercantile Co." Older truck in rear was a Kelly-Springfield, with solid rubber tires. *Lyon County, Kansas, Historical Museum*

Packard, circa 1920s
There was a single high beam running along the center of this beverage stake truck. In the middle was a small signboard, and at the rear sat the three-dimensional figure of a clothed fox. The truck was an early 1920s Packard, and the product was Bevo, a "near-beer" made by Anheuser-Busch. *Anheuser-Busch Archives*

International, circa 1925
A mid-1920s International used by the Herman Gallas & Co. awning and canopies firm. *General Body Co.*

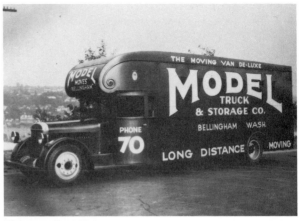

Kenworth, 1928
The metalwork above the cab and on the doors of this 1928 Kenworth was curved. Some early streamlining efforts were also aimed at lowering wind resistance. *Paccar*

International, circa 1925
Detail of construction and lettering along the rear of the body. As the signwriting stated, "We fool the sun." *General Body Co.*

GMC, 1928
The streamlining on this 1928 GMC is seen in the sheet metal extending rearward from the cab, rather than the squat cargo box. This feature has been on expensive models of pickup trucks since the mid-1950s and also was a feature of the Ford Ranchero and Chevrolet El Camino. *Public Archives of Canada*

Studebaker, 1929
A florist had a flower-basket design fitted onto a 1929 Studebaker chassis. *National Automotive History Collection, Detroit Public Library*

White, circa 1930
This moving van was a White tractor-trailer combination from about 1930. The tractor's rear wheels were behind the men. Note how the metalwork on the front tractor blended with that in the trailer's body. The metalwork extended behind the cab and enclosed the metalwork at the front of the trailer. This was necessary for turning. *Volvo/White*

General Body, circa 1930s
The General Body Company's proposal for a streamlined laundry truck in the 1930s. *General Body Co.*

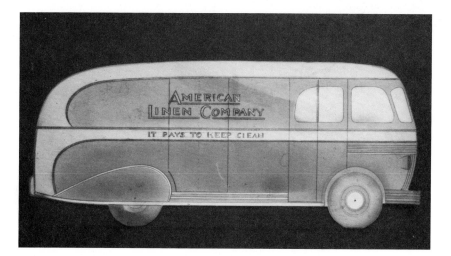

Ford, circa 1930s
A small sign, perhaps temporary, mounted on hood of a late 1930s Ford V-8. *O. V. Hunt Collection, Birmingham Public Library*

General Body, circa 1930s
A streamlined body, from the 1930s, used to carry the Herbie Kay orchestra's band equipment. *General Body Co.*

Chevrolet, 1930
The small cutout was of a telephone and displayed the merchant's phone number. Panel truck was probably a Chevrolet from 1930. *National Grocers Association*

White, circa 1930s
This was an artist's drawing, developed for White in the 1930s, showing a possible streamlined stake truck body. *National Automotive History Collection, Detroit Public Library*

Ford, 1932
This was a 1932 Ford that advertised bubble gum. The banner on the front flagstaff said, "Blony," and a balloon in the mouth of the character on the roof expanded and contracted, looking like a bubble. *Ford Archives*

International, 1933
Note the "Why Drudge?" sign mounted above the driver's compartment on this spiffy 1933 International boulevard delivery, a 1 1/2 ton Model D. Many trucks used for local deliveries, as opposed to intercity highways, often had signs like these that would have caused wind resistance at higher speeds. Note also the lettering on the door saying, "No Passengers." *Navistar Archives*

Mack, 1934
This 1934 Mack tank truck had both a small sign above the cab and large lettering on the sides, extending outward from the curved tank. *Historical Collections, Security Pacific National Bank*

Ford, circa 1935
In the mid-1930s, the Hill Auto Body Metal Works of Cincinnati built six of the streamlined commercial cars on Ford chassis for the McQuay-Norris Co. of St. Louis. McQuay-Norris sold auto parts and used the six autos around the country to both test and promote its products. *Harrah's Automobile Collection, Reno*

Ford, circa 1935
This streamlined body was placed on a mid-1930s Ford chassis. Note the sloping rear of the body and fender skirts. *A.L. Hansen Mfg. Co.*

White, circa 1935
The arrow mounted to metal brackets on the top of this beer truck stated, "It hits the spot." Truck was a mid-1930s White, operated by the Globe Brewery of Baltimore. *National Automotive History Collection, Detroit Public Library*

Mack, circa 1936
The differences between streamlined and unstreamlined are evident when looking at this Cord auto and Mack truck. Car has 1936 license plates. *Baker Library, Harvard University*

Ford, 1936
Duro Metal Products Co. of Chicago used this rig, mounted on a 1936 Ford chassis, as a traveling showroom. *Ford Archives*

International, 1937
A pair of squat buses, apparently benefiting from a "streamlined" paint pattern. Chassis were 1937 Internationals. *Gillig Corporation*

Make unknown, circa 1937
A Canadian beer truck from the late 1930s based on an unknown make of tractor but with a trailer and probably all the streamlining done by Fruehauf. Note especially the enclosed wheels. *Fruehauf*

Baillargeon, circa 1937
J. B. Baillargeon, a Canadian household goods moving firm, built this unit in its own shops in the late 1930s. The streamlining was for both reducing wind resistance and advertising. The rig had distinctive chrome fitting, gold lettering, and was painted royal blue. *Fruehauf*

General Body, circa 1937
General's proposal for a streamlined beer truck in the late 1930s. *General Body Co.*

General Body, circa 1937
A custom body of the late 1930s. *General Body Co.*

Unknown make, circa 1937
Coin-like emblems with an Indian's head were used by the Chief Laundry. *Navistar Archives*

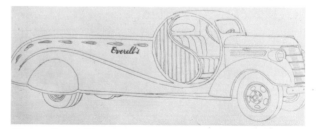

Chevrolet, 1938
W. Everett Miller, the famed truck and auto body designer, made this sketch in 1938 showing a proposed body treatment of a Chevrolet. *Blackhawk Automobile Collection*

White fleet, 1939
Here were two Labatt's beer trucks using streamlined
White tractors and modified Fruehauf trailers.
Labatt's had a fleet of similar, although not identical,
rigs. Some other trailers were more streamlined than
the ones shown here. *Volvo/White*

Mack, circa 1940
Cutouts of Coca-Cola bottles were bolted onto this bot-
tler's stake truck, a Mack from about 1940. *Mack
Museum*

GMC, circa 1940s
Sign on top of a 1940s GMC dry-cleaning truck used in
Washington, D. C. *Smithsonian Institution*

International, circa 1940
This International step-van from about 1940 was used
by a florist. Note both the extruding letters and painted fringe. *Navistar Archives*

Ford, 1940
A streamlined refrigerated trailer, pulled by a 1940
Ford tractor. Note the curvature of the painted trim.
American Body & Equipment Co.

International, 1940
This 1940 International laundry truck had a rack on
top for bags of soiled linens and extra lettering on the
sides of the rack. *Navistar Archives*

Heil, circa 1940s
The rear of a Heil streamlined oil tanker body. *The
Heil Co.*

White, 1940
Cutout letters were mounted on a metal bar attached
to the truck's roof. Rig was a 1940 White. *Volvo/White*

International, circa 1940
A streamlined International tank truck. Headlights were from a 1939 Plymouth. *Navistar Archives*

Mack, circa 1940s
This streamlined truck, on a Mack chassis, was used by Benjamin Moore paints. The circle in the center probably had a rainbow of colors. *Mack Museum*

Ford, 1940
A 1940 Ford bottler's truck. Streamlining included mounting Ford auto headlights at a 90-degree angle. *Kranz Body Co.*

Dodge, circa 1940s
A US brewer's streamlined truck, mounted on a Dodge chassis. *A.L. Hansen Mfg. Co.*

International, circa 1940s
An Iowa furniture store used this International for deliveries. Note the enclosed wheels. *Navistar Archives*

Ford, circa 1970s
Playing with the letters on the front of the cab of this Ford C-series yielded the word ROOF. This truck was used by a roofer.

Chapter 4

Trucks With Special Lights and Sounds

This chapter covers a range of trucks and truck bodies that were specially built or equipped to serve in an advertising function. Many incorporated special lighting or sound units. Interestingly, many of these rigs were used to advertise movies. An article in a 1928 issue of *Motor Truck* began with these words: "Edward R. Wood, of Rochester, New York, was searching for 'something different and high-class' with which to advertise the latest million dollar movie production of *Uncle Tom's Cabin*, when he saw the new Selden sedan de luxe and exclaimed 'That's the thing!' He then wanted to install an organ in it and have the truck engine operate the organ...."

The article then described how he was able to accomplish this—an apparent first—since previously, truck-mounted organs had needed their own power sources.

This chapter shows the range of advertising uses to which trucks have been put. There might be some particular reason why a restorer would want to adapt his or her truck with some of the devices shown here. About the only adaptation the author has seen on restored trucks is the addition of calliopes.

Also included are a few pictures of miniature or "half-size" trucks. These were once widely used by truck lines for promotional purposes. (In late 1984 one such miniature tractor-double-trailer rig consisting of a tractor that was 8ft, 2in long, double trailers each 13ft, 3in long, and a full-sized lowboy trailer for carrying the miniatures was advertised for bidding in *Wheels of Time*.)

White, 1906
This 1906 White carried a boiler to generate steam for rug cleaning; the steam was also used for powering the pipe organ seen on the side. *Volvo/White*

Make unknown, circa 1920s
This truck from the early 1920s appears to be made for carrying advertising. The side panels were over-sized, and the top of the truck body and cab carried rows of small lights. *American Truck Historical Society*

Wichita, circa 1905
This Wichita truck was truly a traveling billboard. The vertical slats were three-sided, and rotated, making it possible to show three different messages. *Railway Negative Exchange*

Reincarnated hearse, circa 1920s
This truck, possibly a reincarnated hearse, had speakers and an illuminated sign. It was used to promote a San Francisco nightclub. The lines on the back and side suggest that it was painted with a variety of colors. *California State Archives*

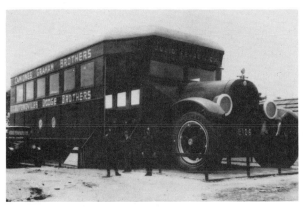

Graham Bros., circa 1920s
The opposite of miniature trucks would be oversized ones. Here was a replica of a Graham Bros., with front tires nearly 10ft high, being used in a Latin American fair. The truck on left was regular size. *National Automotive History Collection, Detroit Public Library*

International, circa 1925
This mid-1920s International, with comfortable chairseats placed in a circular pattern in the rear, had two rearward facing loudspeakers. The unit was used by the Cotton Belt Railroad. *Navistar Archives*

Kenworth, 1928
This late 1928 Kenworth had a small, illuminated sign box above its cab. *Paccar*

Kenworth, 1928
Detail of the intricate paint scheme on the Kenworth advertising Gold Shield Coffee. *Paccar*

International, circa 1930s
The sign on the side of this 1930s International stated, "Standard Oil Announcer Service." It may have been used at races. *Standard Oil of California*

Pierce-Arrow, 1929
A Pierce-Arrow carrying a heavy I-beam. Small lights illuminated the load and its message.

Pierce-Arrow, circa 1930s
Two small floodlights at the top front, just above the cab, illuminated the words "Holmes, Fresno" on this Pierce-Arrow moving van. *Smithsonian Institution*

Mack, circa 1930s
Werner Transportation Company used this miniature Mack alongside a full-sized rig to promote its moving prowess.

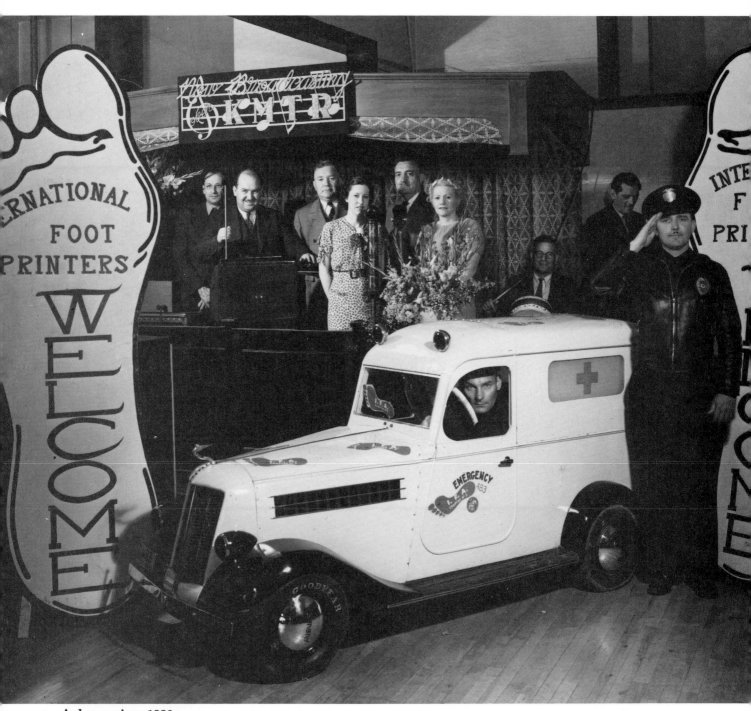

Auburn, circa 1930s
A miniature Auburn ambulance. *Whittington Collection, California State University, Long Beach*

Austin, 1930
This 1930 Austin with speakers on top was used to promote Chinese food (made in "Spotless American Kitchens"). Note the giant-sized product can mounted on the right front fender. *Whittington Collection, California State University, Long Beach*

GMC, 1932
Thanks to an old press release provided by Gerber, we know more than usual about this set of double trailers pulled by a 1932 GMC tractor. The combined length of all three units was 58ft (this was before some states limited lengths). According to the press release, it was at that time the largest vehicle ever painted with duco—thirteen coats no less—"which give it as fine a finish as the finest car.... Delicately painted in blue and white, the giant unit is an unusually pleasing sight, particularly at night with all of the red and green lights glowing that are prescribed by law, and the additional lights that have been added for display value at night time." Close examination of the picture showed these lights, and the truck was shown as it appeared at night. *Gerber*

80

Mack, 1934
A 1934 Mack (the streamlined body was designed by
W. Everett Miller), used by Gilmore Oil Co. of Los
Angeles, covered with neon tubing. Note the neon tubing over the cab. (One wonders what a present-day
insurance company's reaction would be to a truck covered with neon tubing.) *Mack Museum*

Chevrolet, circa 1935
The spare-tire cover on this mid-1930s Chevrolet
enclosed a revolving sign that advertised Wrigley's
gum. *Wm. J. Wrigley, Jr. Co.*

Chevrolet, circa 1935
This mid-1930s Chevrolet was probably used by a
traveling preacher. On stage, one can see a micro-
phone and organ keyboard. *Kranz Body Co.*

Chevrolet, circa 1935
Loudspeakers were mounted on top of this truck; pictures on the side of the body showed various home
appliances. Truck was a mid-1930s Chevrolet. *National Automotive History Collection, Detroit Public
Library*

White, circa 1935
The cowl at the top front of this trailer protected the
lights that illuminated the signs below. They could be
seen by oncoming traffic and pedestrians. Truck was a
White from the mid-1930s and was used by Kroger.
Lighting of this sort caused problems with the drain it
placed on the vehicle's electrical-generating system.
Kroger

Neon car, 1937
Throughout the late 1930s, advertising magazines had pictures and brief articles about autos and trucks with neon tubing attached. Portions of their discussion dealt with provision of generators and transformers needed to sustain the systems. Neon signs mounted on autos were used mainly to promote new autos, such as this 1937 Oldsmobile. *Harrah's Automobile Collection, Reno*

Neon car, 1938
Neon signs on autos were also used to promote other products, such as Calvert whiskies. Seen at the Cheyenne, Wyoming, Frontier Days in 1938, these fellows seemed anxious to get away from the camera and follow the neon advice—"Clever heads call for Calvert Whiskies."

Trailer, 1938
This trailer was a traveling billboard for promoting movies; the theater's name was in neon on the top. *California State Archives*

Mack, circa 1940s
Here's the "Johnson Junior" miniature Mack truck and attendant trailer used to promote a motor carrier. Celebrity Arthur Godfrey stands at left. *American Trucking Associations*

Diamond-T, 1948
The words "Ed. Clark" on top of this 1948 Diamond-T were studded with small button reflectors to be picked up in the headlights of oncoming traffic. *Mike Pagel*

Truck billboard, circa 1950s
A large truck figure, once used as a billboard in the New York City area. *W.A. Drew*

Chevrolet, circa 1955
This mid 1950s Chevrolet panel had fold-down loudspeakers mounted on its roof to sing the virtues of Jif peanut butter to youngsters everywhere. *Proctor & Gamble*

Chapter 5

Productmobiles

"Even before the cries of 'Get a horse' died down and the automobile had become firmly established, a few companies saw an opportunity to capitalize on the motorcar with special promotional bodies. Shaped like the product they advertised, these vehicles drew attention wherever they went. For want of a better term, I'll call these cars 'productmobiles.'"

—Automotive historian Roy I. Scroggins, writing in *Special-Interest Autos,* 1976

Productmobiles are vehicles with bodies shaped to represent the product they were supposed to promote. Most of them are associated with the period before World War II when labor and materials were relatively cheap. George Barris, who also builds unique vehicles for use in the movie industry, is often associated with the occasional productmobiles that are still being built today.

The March 1931 issue of *The Automobile Trimmer and Painter* contains a five-page article with drawings showing how to build a shoe-shaped delivery vehicle. The article says, in part, "A desirable keynote in connection with light delivery trucks is that of building the delivery body to represent something the owner sells...."

Puffed rice demonstrator, 1910
This rig demonstrated how puffed cereal was "shot from guns." *Quaker Oats*

Thermos-mobile, circa 1910
This early productmobile was a Thermos bottle tipped on its side. One wheel was painted with "keeps hot," the other, "keeps cold." *National Automotive History Collection, Detroit Public Library*

Chewing gum wagon, circa 1900
Productmobiles date from before the auto; here's a horse-drawn rig that looked like a package of chewing gum.

Maybe the dealer who orders the body sells canned goods of some particular brand he wishes to push. Then build the delivery body in the form of a tin can lying on its side. Maybe it's bottled goods he sells.... There's an idea to follow up. Build the body in the shape of some characteristic bottle that contains his wares. Paint it accordingly, playing up the label.

"Following this line of thought, you can profit without a doubt, for businessmen everywhere recognize the value of distinctive advertising. Idealists tell us our nation is addicted to over-advertising. Maybe that's true.... But, as long as you're in the stream you've nearly *got* to swim with the current. So nearly every business man realizes that if he's going to *sell* what he has to sell he must advertise—and plenty."

I grew up in Madison, Wisconsin, where the headquarters of Oscar Mayer is located, and I recall seeing its Wienermobile—a 20ft-long wiener on four wheels. Actually, there was a series of Weinermobiles, starting in the mid-1930s and built up to the present time, using metal and fiberglass-reinforced plastic. A small man (named "Little Oscar") rode in or drove the vehicle and at trade shows would dispense cocktail sausages or small wiener-shaped whistles. Oscar Mayer Wienermobiles are still in use.

Very few productmobiles remain; some are in museums. A number of pictures of productmobiles are included here since they would have to be considered the ultimate truck to use for product promotion.

Bread loaf on wheels, circa 1910
This early truck was fitted with a bread-loaf-shaped
body. *Maine Historic Preservation Commission*

Ford Model T, circa 1915
This Model T Ford had a camera-like body. Inside was
a real photographer who would snap pictures of people
at fairs. *Hews Body Co.*

Ford Model T, circa 1915
The Chattanooga Beverage Company placed a bottle
on the back of a Ford Model T to promote Bevo, a
"near-beer." *Anheuser-Busch Archives*

Ford Model T,
A Ford Model T coupe with a large piston mounted on the trunk to promote Simplex piston rings. *Weber's, Fort Worth*

Packard, circa 1917
A parade float promoting milk based on a Packard chassis, circa 1915–1920. *Skagit County Historical Museum*

Life Saver truck, 1918
A 1918 Ford with a body shaped like the Life Savers it
was used to promote.

Ford Model T, circa 1920
This Los Angeles picture shows a Ford Model T used

by a supplier of prefabricated houses. *The Whittington
Collection, California State University, Long Beach*

Chevrolet, circa 1920
A shoe-shaped productmobile on an early 1920s
Chevrolet chassis. *Weber's, Fort Worth*

Torpedo wagons, circa 1920
Torpedo-sized cigars were mounted on the tops of the
trucks used to deliver Muriel Cigars. *Navistar
Archives*

Dodge, 1921
This 1921 Dodge was used by an Atlantic City photographer. *Library of Philadelphia*

90

Daimler, circa 1925
This is a German-built Daimler truck used to advertise an ale. It was photographed at the National Motor Museum at Beaulieu, England.

Ford Model AA, circa 1930
A Ford Model AA with a load that looks like an auto battery. *National Automotive History Collection, Detroit Public Library*

White, 1930
A lumber company in St. Louis used this body for advertising. It was built on a 1930 White 65 chassis. *Volvo/White*

Cadillac, 1930
Not exactly a truck, this 1930 Cadillac was outfitted to promote a soft drink. Note the steering wheel; the complicated levers and linkages were employed to bring all of the auto's controls within reach of the driver. Several of these units were built; one still exists. *The Whittington Collection, California State University, Long Beach*

Shoemobile, 1931
This drawing of a shoe-shaped vehicle appeared in a 1931 issue of *The Automobile Trimmer and Painter*, which described how to build a shoe shop delivery truck. *Harrah's Automobile Collection, Reno*

Bromo-Seltzer wagon, 1932
This 1932 White was used to promote Bromo-Seltzer.

Ford, 1935
A 1935 Ford with a milk-bottle body advertising Borden's Golden Crest Grade A Milk. *Ford Archives*

Soupmobile, circa 1935
This mid-1930s Dodge was fitted with a giant soup can at midship. *Chrysler Historical Archives*

Diamond-T, 1937
A 1937 3/4 ton Diamond-T Model 80 Deluxe with a battery-like cargo box including terminals on top. *Mike Pagel*

Ford, 1941
A 1941 Ford with a cask used to promote a restaurant named the "Cask'n Cleaver."

Ford, 1949
A 1949 Ford auto with a large glass canning jar mounted on the trunk. *Heiser*

Milk carton on wheels, circa 1950
An early 1950s Dodge with a body shaped like milk cartons. *General Body Co.*

Milk carton on wheels, circa 1950
Close-up shows rear the hardware and lights. *General Body Co.*

Teapot van, circa 1950s
This was a relatively unsophisticated productmobile. The step-van was converted to look like a teapot by adding a spout and handle. *Historical Society of Western Pennsylvania*

Teapot van, circa 1950s
The handle protruded from the rear doors—and must have been handy for opening the left-hand one! *Historical Society of Western Pennsylvania*

Bread loaf on wheels, 1959
A VW van painted to look like a loaf of Valley Pride
Bread. *Valley Baking Company, Shippensburg, PA*

Weinermobile, circa 1960s
A later Oscar Mayer Wienermobile with an enclosed
cab. *Oscar Mayer*

96

Weinermobile, circa 1960s
An early Oscar Mayer Wienermobile with an odd cab mounted on top, detracting from the weiner-shaped lines. *Oscar Mayer*

Weinermobile, circa 1960s
Construction of the later Oscar Mayer Wienermobile.
Gerstenslager

Muffler-mobile, circa 1960s
A muffler shop used this productmobile. *Roy Stewart*

Lemon van, date unknown
This productmobile was shaped and
colored like a lemon. It was photographed at the National Motor
Museum at Beaulieu, England.

Chevrolet, 1988
The productmobile idea survives;
this Chevrolet was photographed at
a Reno rodeo in 1988.

Chapter 6

Showing the Goods

The trucks pictured in this chapter were used for the sole purpose of displaying products. Some were used by wholesalers as they made calls on retailers; some were used for trade shows; and some were traveling retail showrooms. It's difficult to know for certain exactly how some of the trucks were used, however, we doubt that products were sold directly off of the trucks. At most, orders were taken.

Aside from the pictures, relatively little is known about these trucks. Bus bodies were frequently used if one wanted sufficient height so that customers could walk around inside the truck. An article from a 1931 trade journal

Household goods vendor, circa 1910
This picture, taken before 1910, shows a truck used by a household goods wholesaler to display his wares. *Connecticut Historical Society*

Ford Model T, circa 1917
This Model T Ford was used to demonstrate overhead garage doors, and it had one installed on its rear. *Todco*

described a body built in New England for use by a wholesale firm that handled seeds, garden implements, and lawn supplies. The inside measurements were between six and seven feet wide (in those times truck bodies and cabs tended to be narrower at the front), fifteen feet in length, and seven feet in height. Customer entrance was through a right front door, but there was also a larger rear opening through which equipment and displays would be loaded.

This chapter has several purposes. Individual interested in the use of trucks for advertising can get a look at some very specialized body types. In a historical sense, one can see how trucks were used to display many of the wares that industry was providing for consumers. Individuals contemplating the use of an old, restored truck for advertising purposes might be able to get "more bangs for the buck" by copying a use

such as this, since they would be able to display their specific products (old or new) in addition to advertising them.

White, circa 1917
This World War I-vintage White was used to display railroad signs and lanterns. *Volvo/White*

Ford Model T, circa 1920s
This Ford Model T with a custom radiator shell displayed an early Hoover vacuum cleaner, or "Suction Sweeper," behind glass. The truck was part of a fleet used by repairmen in the early 1920s. The fleet was abandoned in 1924 as branch service offices were opened. *The Hoover Company*

Unknown make, circa 1925
When was the last time you saw an IBM salesperson in a rig like this? Display Car #72 featured "Dayton Scales, Electric Coffee Mills, Meat Choppers, Slicers, etc., International Time Recorders and Electrical Time Systems, Electric Tabulating and Accounting Machines." *Navistar Archives*

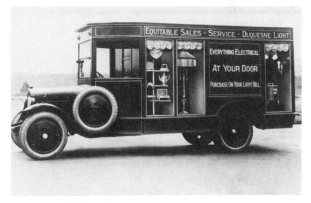

Graham Bros., circa 1925
This Graham Bros. truck from the mid-1920s was used by an electric utility company to promote sale and use of electrical appliances and lights. The lowest lettering stated, "Purchase on your light bill." *Duquesne Light, Pittsburgh*

Coolerator truck, circa 1925
A Coolerator icebox salesman used this display truck to call at the homes of potential customers. Block ice was fed into the upper compartment of the Coolerator and cool air traveled downward; the pan in the bottom needed periodic draining. *Oregon Historical Society*

White, 1927
Crane plumbing fixtures were displayed in this 1927 White Model 50B, which covered the Miami district. *Volvo/White*

White, 1927
Inside the White display truck, all of Crane's plumbing ware were on show—including a tiled bathroom floor. *Volvo/White*

Ford Model AA, 1931
The California Dairy Council used this Model AA Ford to carry cows and calves to show at fairs. The panels promoted the council ("The cow, the foster mother of the world") and doubled as unloading ramps when lowered. *The Whittington Collection, California State University, Long Beach*

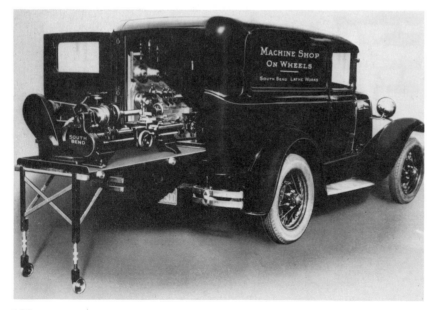

Ford Model AA, 1931
With ramps down, cows and calves were on display. From left, Winnie, Dimple, and two unknowns. *The Whittington Collection, California State University, Long Beach*

Ford Model A, circa 1925
The floor of this Ford Model A panel was modified so that a display frame could be extended to the rear where the lathe was accessible. *National Automotive History Collection, Detroit Public Library*

Graham Bros., circa 1927
This Graham Bros. truck from the late 1920s was used for displaying hand tools. Note the attractive painting on panel sides. *National Automotive History Collection, Detroit Public Library*

Graham Bros., circa 1927
The roof expanded upward and the sides extended outward, features that can be found on camping trailers and vans today. *National Automotive History Collection, Detroit Public Library*

Dodge, circa 1930
This Dodge from about 1930 displayed a room of patio furniture—"The Way to Happy Homes." Note the bus-like firm sign above windshield. *Chrysler Historical Collection*

Ford, circa 1932
This early Ford V-8 canopied pickup displayed a V-8 engine block and related parts. It was a true rolling billboard, powered by its own wares. *Ford Archives*

Federal, circa 1935
The Shaw Fish Company had a mid-1930s Federal truck with aquarium-like tanks on each side filled with swimming fish. *Motor Vehicle Manufacturers Association*

Chevrolet, 1935
This 1935 Chevrolet coupe had a fifth wheel inserted, and was used to pull an Aerocar trailer that displayed Crosley radios. *National Automotive History Collection, Detroit Public Library*

Dodge, 1935
Standard Oil Company of California used this 1935 Dodge to carry a demonstration kitchen to promote the use of its Flamo fuel. Note the Venetian blinds. *Standard Oil Company of California*

Ford, circa 1937
A late 1930s Ford used to demonstrate General Electric arc-welding gear. The chassis was from a Ford V-8. *General Electric*

International, circa 1937
The Union hardware wholesaler used this late 1930s International as a demonstrator and delivery truck. It was photographed on location in Madison, Wisconsin. *Navistar Archives*

White, 1938
This 1938 White chassis carried a custom, streamlined display body. Note also the plain, oversized hubcaps and the painting scheme above the wheels. *Volvo/White*

Dodge, 1939
This Dodge step-van from about 1939 was used by a plumbing and heating contractor. Visible on the truck's right side were seven compartment doors, raised lettering, and a small window that displayed plumbing fixtures in a tiled setting. *Vintage Motor Sales, Willmar, Minnesota*

Dodge, 1939
Inside the small side window, the plumbing fixtures were set in a tiled sink for demonstration. *Vintage Motor Sales, Willmar, Minnesota*

Autocar, 1940
This 1940 Autocar rig was used to display Dr. Scholl's foot care products. *Dr. Scholl's*

International, 1940
Ohio Edison used this 1940 International panel truck to pull a trailer for demonstrating appliances to farms. Note the streamlined painting patterns on both truck and trailer. *Navistar Archives*

Chevrolet, 1948
This 1948 Chevrolet chassis had a delivery body made of clear plastic. While its initial purpose was to demonstrate truck bodies, the truck saw some actual use by a florist. Drivers said that it was top-heavy. *San Francisco Public Library*

Unknown make, circa 1950s
The Square D Company used this truck to show its
line of switches and panels. *Gerstenslager*

Unknown make, circa 1950s
Inside, the Square D Company truck featured a full
selection of switches and panels. *Gerstenslager*

Ford Ranchero, 1959
Gerstenslager Corporation outfitted this 1959 Ford Ranchero so it could display the Bellows Air Motors' product line. *Gerstenslager*

Chapter 7

Peddling One's Wares

Over the years trucks have been—and still are—used for direct sales or vending to individuals. The truck goes to intersections or into neighborhoods, and customers walk up to it and make their purchase. The best examples today are the canteen or lunch trucks that call on a regular basis at work sites, and the "Good Humor" ice cream trucks that operate in the summer months.

One contemporary use of old trucks is by vendors at flea markets, who store their wares in old trucks during the week and then drive to flea

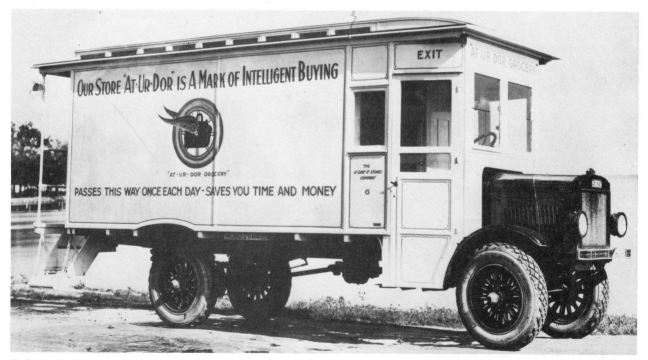

Oshkosh, 1920
This traveling "At-Ur-Door Grocery" store was mounted on a high Oshkosh all-wheel-drive chassis. Cus-

tomers entered from the rear, exited from the front. *Oshkosh Truck Corporation*

White, 1920
A traveling Rexall drug store used in Indianapolis, Indiana, mounted on a 1920 White chassis. Note the bean grinder attached to the inside of the left rear door. *Volvo/White*

markets on weekends. The old trucks may help attract some customers; in any event, they are sufficiently "funky" to fit into flea market decor. That is, flea market vendors don't want to appear to be too prosperous.

A related use of trucks that has all but disappeared from the American scene is that of home deliveries performed by driver/salesperson. The driver/salesperson, paid on a commission basis (also called a route salesperson), made scheduled home deliveries. These trades developed before the auto and lasted until after World War II. Examples of products delivered by driver/salesperson included milk and other dairy goods, bread, ice, laundry, and dry cleaning. The driver/salesperson would also make some cash sales from the truck. (The driver/salesperson continues in some wholesale trades.) In addition to home deliveries, there were also traveling stores, which would operate on regular urban and rural routes.

The popcorn wagon vending truck still attracts great collector interest. Cretors, which built horse-drawn units, stationary units, and units fitted on the rear of trucks, is the best-known maker of popcorn wagons. Today, old Cretors rigs in working order are quite expensive. *Hemmings Motor News*, the publisher of several old car periodicals, uses a "replica" Cretors popcorn body built from original Cretors patterns and dies. Popcorn wagons can be useful for advertising, since the smell of popcorn always attracts a crowd.

Using restored vending trucks for advertising purposes presents an opportunity as well as a possible problem, however. Since these trucks were designed to dispense products, the public might be disappointed to find that they are no longer functioning.

117

White, 1920
A traveling Rexall drug store. Interior shot shows samples attached to the walls; they were probably stocked in the cabinets below. *Volvo/White*

International, circa 1925
Traveling medicine salesmen often used trucks—as this truck's advertising reminded you, "Health is Worth more than Money." This mid-1920s International was used by the maker of "Dr. Hayssen's Famous Goitre Ointment." *Navistar Archives*

Moreland, circa 1925
This "Store at your Door" was mounted on a 1 1/2 ton Moreland chassis, built in southern California. Note the design of the side walls and how the shelves were kept at chest height. The lower ones were accessed while the customer was outside the truck, standing on the ground; the upper ones were reached while the customer was inside the truck. *Library, University of California, Los Angeles*

Moreland, circa 1925
Interior of the Moreland "Store at your Door" with shelving stretching up to the roof. *Library, University of California, Los Angeles*

Fargo, circa 1928
A Fargo (similar to a Dodge) truck from the late 1920s. Note how the drawers pulled out in the rear. Glass windows on the side of the truck's panel enclosed real tools. *National Automotive History Collection, Detroit Public Library*

Graham Bros., 1926
A 1926 Graham Bros. chassis, fitted out with a traveling market body. It's difficult to know what product was being sold; it would have been dispensed through the side openings. *Richard Quinn*

Circular tray display, 1930
This 1930 photo shows a circular tray used for carrying many small parts in a truck. *Motor Vehicle Manufacturers Association*

White, 1931
Here was a Borden's driver/salesman making home deliveries and sales of milk, using a 1931 White with a step-van body. *Volvo / White*

White, 1932
The Ohio Brass Company had fold-down sides on this

1932 White. Cabinets under the display racks held stock. *Volvo/White*

REO, 1934
Through the windows of this REO one can see a mechanical, small-scale circus with moving replicas of

Beech Nut products. There was a vending counter on the other side. Chassis was a 1934 REO. *Beech Nut*

Ford Model AA, circa 1935
A Ford Model AA with a wooden cask-like body used for selling orange drink. *Sam LaRoue*

Ford Model AA, circa 1935
A large popcorn truck on a Ford Model AA chassis. *Allen Kenney*

122

Chevrolet fleet, 1936
A fleet of 1936 Chevrolet "Good Humor" ice cream trucks. *Baker Library, Harvard University*

White, 1939
Shopping "The Modern Way." This 1939 photo, taken in Los Angeles, shows a traveling baked goods sales truck on a White step-van chassis. *Volvo/White*

White, 1939
Interior of the White step-van travelling bakery. *Volvo/White*

Dodge, circa 1940
This picture, taken around 1940, shows a traveling store in rural Arkansas. It was built on a Dodge chassis. On the tailgate were cases of empty soft drink bottles and a barrel for dispensing kerosene. *National Archives*

Chevrolet El Camino, 1960
A 1960 Chevrolet El Camino used by a flea market vendor.

Chevrolet, circa 1965
A step-van body on a mid-1960s Chevrolet chassis used for selling Hood's ice cream. *Union City Body Co.*

Chapter 8

Today's Use of Old Trucks for Advertising

Up until this point, we have discussed old trucks and their uses for advertising. The photographs in this chapter show some "tie-ins" or reinforcements that some firms use to repeat the theme created by their old truck. From an advertising standpoint, it is considered necessary to repeat one's message time and time again. Illustrations will be of these "tie-ins," although in some instances the firm using the "tie-in" may or may not actually own a full-sized old truck or bus.

Old trucks—or the "old truck idea"—are often incorporated into advertising. For example, a number of young men's outdoor fashion ads that appear in print often show a 1950s pickup in the background, and old trucks (and cars) are frequently used on TV commercials.

Individuals contemplating restoring an old truck and using it for advertising should give careful thought toward finding ways to reinforce the advertising theme they plan to adopt. This is necessary in order to obtain fuller value from one's advertising expenditures.

Willys Jeep display
This old military Jeep was mounted half inside and half outside a specially cut plate glass window at the front a Banana Republic store located in a suburban Miami shopping center.

Ford Model A
Everbrite Electric Signs of South Milwaukee found this old photo of one of its Ford Model As, and they incorporated the photo into a full-color brochure directed at new clients. *Everbrite*

126

Grade A Grade Crossings.

COBRA X®Grade Crossing Modules are durable, versatile, economical and smooth riding.

COBRA X modular, interlocking railroad grade crossings are made of high-density polyethylene that can take heavy loads and high traffic volume with ease. And that's how they ride, too. Easy.

Low-maintenance COBRA X Modules are resistant to abrasion, moisture, road shocks, potholes and splinters. They are available in various heights and are suitable for use on tangent tracks and curves.

Since you can buy our Grade A crossings for less money than equivalent products, why not specify COBRA X?

For information on our five-year warranty, write Railroad Friction Products Corporation, Wilmerding, PA 15148. Or phone: 412/824-8890. In Canada, write COBRA Canada, Inc.,
P. O. Box 2050,
Hamilton, Ontario
L8N 3T5.

Chevrolet pickup ad
An ad for steel grade crossings featuring an old truck.

Dudreck, DePaul, Ficco, & Morgan Advertising, Pittsburgh

127

1908

1910 WHITE

1910 KELLY

ALLIED VAN LINES.INC
LONG DISTANCE MOVING
FORD STORAGE & MOVING CO
OMAHA, NEBRASKA

1958

Allied van lines card
The cover of a card used some time ago by a Council Bluffs moving company to advertise its fiftieth anniversary. *R. A. Ford*

Mack toy truck
During the holiday season in 1985, Texaco dealers sold a Mack tank truck bank, shown on the lower right.

Dodge restaurant bar
A late 1920s Dodge used in a Southern California restaurant.

Dodge restaurant bar
A food eating counter has been built around the flatbed of the 1920s Dodge.

American LaFrance
The Hall of Flame Museum in Phoenix had this early 1920s American LaFrance pumper for kids to play on and pose on for pictures.

Doane toy truck
It's possible to have one-of-a-kind scale models built for promotional purposes. Here's a model of a Doane lowbed pulling a one-time horse-drawn wagon, produced by Clive T. Jones of Edmonton, Alberta. *Clive T. Jones*

Ford and Chevrolet toy trucks
At an old car flea market, a vendor was selling these models of a Ford Model T and an early 1950s Chevrolet truck. Both had "True Value" store markings.

Ford toy truck
Bird Automotive of Omaha built these child-size 1911 Ford replicas. This one has Dr. Pepper markings.

The Dr Pepper 1911 replica old time delivery truck features a wooden box, 3 hp motor, spoke wheels and speed of approximately 15 mph.

131

Step-van toy truck
Classic Motorbooks had some of these small (about 7in long) step-vans made to celebrate its twentieth anniversary.

Toy trucks
Ertl bank replicas of old trucks with markings of older firms. *The Ertl Company*

Toy truck
A new cast-metal toy, modeled after those of the 1920s. Markings are for Malatesta & Sons, a firm that still exists.

Toy trucks
Ertl bank replicas of new trucks with markings of present-day firms. *The Ertl Company*

BARTLES & JAYMES
WINE COOLER
"INTRO"

:30 Commercial

FRANK: Well, the new Bartles and Jaymes premium wine cooler . . .

is finally in the bottle . . .

and our marketing director, Gary Cox is now getting ready . . .

to put it into distribution in major markets. Please buy some, because frankly . . .

from our point of view there's no other wine cooler anywhere that's nearly as good at any price.

It would also be a personal favor to Ed, because he took out that second on his house . . .

and pretty soon he's got a big balloon payment coming up. Thank you and we hope you enjoy your new premium wine cooler.

Bartles & Jaymes ad
A reproduction of a TV commercial storyboard showing the text and seven shots. Featured in the background was a red 1948 Ford pickup with the sponsor's name painted on the door. *E. & J. Gallo Winery*

134

Telephone truck toys
The Yorkshire Company of Glen Ellyn, Illinois, made these small replicas of telephone trucks. Some were sold as desk pen holders.

Dart tilework
Dart Trucks were built in Kansas City, Missouri, and this tiled work—showing Dart's first truck—was on an

Specialty Vehicles repli-bus
These vehicles are called "repli-buses." They were made of modern parts on new truck and bus chassis. Only the sheet metal design was "old-fashioned," based on vehicles in style at the turn of the century.

Vehicles such as these are an alternative for a firm wanting to capture an "old" theme yet have a modern vehicle manufactured to today's standards. This repli-bus was built by the Specialty Vehicles Corporation of Zellwood, Florida. *Specialty Vehicles Corp.*

Federal repli-bus
A repli-bus built by Federal Motors of Ocala, Florida.
Federal Motors

Chapter 9

1900-1929 Vintage Commercial Trucks

Many pictures of restored trucks appear in this chapter, and readers will note a large number of Fords. This is for several reasons. First of all, in the years prior to 1930, Ford built approximately half the trucks sold in the United States; hence we should expect a large number of survivors. Second, and as will be discussed in chapter 12, it is relatively easy to find parts for restoration of a Ford Model T or Model A, hence they make good candidates for successful

REO, 1905
Sterling Transit Company, a trucking firm based in southern California, has several old trucks, including this 1905 REO.

REO, 1905
Close-up of the REO shows the chain drive and lettering along the side of the box.

restoration. Third, from an editorial standpoint, we included Ford Model As in this chapter, even though the model spanned the years 1928-1931.

REO, 1911
This 1911 Reo sat in the entryway of the offices of Osterlund Trucks in Harrisburg, Pennsylvania, which builds Giant Trucks, a descendent of the REO line. *Osterlund, Inc.*

Ford, 1909
A 1909 Ford C-cab panel parked next to a newer Ford dump truck. *Western Reserve*

Ford Model T, 1909
American Red Ball Transit Company of Indianapolis, Indiana, used this 1909 Ford Model T. The hood and fenders were red, the body white, and the trim gold. *American Red Ball*

Federals, 1912 and 1946
This picture, taken in 1946, shows a 1912 Federal (one of the first built) that had been restored by the Federal Motor Truck Company. Next to it was a 1946 Federal. The firm produced trucks until 1959. *American Truck Historical Society*

Johnson, 1911
Early in its life, Johnson Controls, Inc., of Milwaukee, Wisconsin, built Johnson trucks. One of its first models, built in 1911, was tracked down and restored by company employees. This 1984 picture shows the truck and the employees who helped restore it.

Ford Model T, 1913
United Parcel Service keeps several restored old trucks in different parts of the country. This is its 1913 Ford Model T that has been in the Macy's Thanksgiving Day parade in New York and on TV. UPS also ran a TV commercial that featured this—or a similar—truck. *UPS*

White, 1913, and Autocar, 1960
A 1913 White and a 1960 Autocar, both owned by the Tucson Warehouse & Transfer Company. *Volvo/White*

Selden, 1914
Sterling Transit's 1914 Selden.

Greyhound's fleet

Greyhound has a fleet of restored buses, including its first rig, which was little more than an automobile—a 1914 Hupmobile, shown on the far right. Working our way to the left, we see a 1931 Mack bus, a 1937 Super Coach, the 1947 Silversides, the 1948 ACF Brill, and a 1954 Scenicruiser. According to a company press release, "The bus classics appear throughout the country at numerous parades and special events. The drivers wear vintage uniforms appropriate to each era." *Greyhound*

Ford, 1914

Wise Ford Lincoln Mercury of Hazlehurst, Mississippi, owned several Ford Model T cars and trucks. This 1914 Ford open coupe had been originally sold by the firm to a customer in 1914. *John D. Wise, Jr.*

Ford, 1914, and White, 1917
Harris Transportation Company of Victorville, California, used this picture on a postcard. At far left was a 1914 Ford. Next to it was a 1917 White similar to the one used in the company's early days. *Harris Transportation*

Ford Model A, circa 1915
Hemmings Motor News used this restored Model A with a popcorn body for fund-raising events. The photo shows Hemmings' staffers handing over the "take" of the day's popcorn sales to representatives of the Vermont Symphony Orchestra. *Hemmings Motor News*

Cretors, 1915
A 1915 Cretors popcorn wagon once in use at Harrah's
automobile collection in Reno.

Packard, circa 1915
A restored Packard truck with an elaborate advertising sign. *Ontario Trucking Association*

144

Ford Model T, circa 1915
This early Ford Model T was used to promote "Italian Dry Salame" in the San Francisco area.

Ford Model T, 1917
Shown on a trailer where it had been hauled for a parade was this truck belonging to John's IGA markets in Blair and Black River Falls, Wisconsin. The lettering on the side of the cab stated, "1917 Model T Ford."

Ford, 1917
This 1917 Ford was one of several old trucks restored by Coles Express in Bangor, Maine. *Galen Cole*

Ford Model T, circa 1917
This Ford Model T was used by a Colorado Springs firm that sold old and restored automobiles. *House of Cars*

Ford, 1917, and GMC, 1946
Michaud Bus Lines of Salem, Massachusetts, has restored both the 1917 Ford and the 1946 GMC (on the right). Picture is from a postcard Michaud distributed. *Michaud Bus Lines*

Ford Model T, circa 1917
This restored Ford Model T had an extended frame and carried bottled water. *Ephrata Diamond Spring Water Co.*

Unknown make, circa 1917
A World War I-era truck, probably ex-military, carrying a water tank and parked so it can advertise a retail store in western Nevada.

Oshkosh, 1917
Oshkosh Truck Corporation used its first four-wheel-drive truck, dating from 1917, to pose with a military rig it built seventy-five years later. *Oshkosh Truck Corporation*

Selden, 1919
A restoration of the original 1919 Selden moving van used by Von Paris Moving & Storage of Timonium, Maryland. *George H. von Paris*

Seagrave, circa 1920s
This early 1920s Seagrave fire engine was used by San Francisco's Red Garter Saloon. Here it's shown in 1981 in a local parade, carrying both an organ and videotape equipment.

Chevrolet, 1920
On the left is a restored 1920 Chevrolet, one of the earliest Chevy trucks. It's shown next to a Turbo truck that Chevrolet was promoting. *Chevrolet*

International, circa 1920
An early 1920s International, used by Fredrickson Motor Express of Charlotte, North Carolina. The truck was similar to the 1919 International used by the company's founder. According to the company, the restored truck "has a venerable role as a Fredrickson Motor Express 'spokesman.' The public sees Old No. 1 in parades, at antique car shows, at colleges, at high school career days and at other events, especially ones involving children. It's not just shut away in a showcase. When we take it out, we let the kids climb all over it, and they love it." *Fredrickson Motor Express Corp.*

Doane, circa 1920s
An early 1920s Doane restored for the Seattle Transfer and Storage Company. *Heiser*

Mack, 1920
A Mack from about 1920 used by
Eady Construction Company of
Louisville, Kentucky, in a parade.
Richard P. Downs

International, 1920
A 1920 International tank truck,
restored by Merrill Transport Company in Portland, Maine.

Ford Model T, 1920
This 1920 Ford Model T, owned by Ed Archer, promotes Dreyer's Ice Cream, made in northern California.

REO, 1921
A 1921 REO one-ton stake truck, restored and used by Semple Truck Leasing in Boston.

Ford Model A, circa 1920s
Popcorn wagon on a Ford Model A chassis.

Doane, 1922
Doane trucks were built in San Francisco. They were lowbeds and used to transport bagged coffee beans and other cargoes from pier to pier. This was a 1922 Doane, restored by the National Truck School of San Rafael, California. The slogan on the top cover said, "Keep On Truckin'."

Fords, 1922 and 1932
Two old trucks used by Christian Schmidt Brewing Company of Philadelphia. At left was a circa-1922 Ford; at right, a 1932 Ford Model B (displaying a pyramid of 12oz beer cans). The accompanying press release indicated that the sign work on both trucks had been redone to feature the company's new logo. *Romm & Karetny*

Mack Bulldog, 1922
A 1922 Mack Bulldog restored, painted bright red, and used as a parade piece by Smith Transportation Company of Santa Maria, California. The company prepared a four-color brochure describing the truck and its restoration that ends with this statement: "This splendid restoration is equipped with a sixteen-foot flat-rack body that is ideal for parade work carrying floats or displays and is available without cost, to any recognized civic group in the Ventura, Santa Barbara or San Luis Obispo Counties."

Ford, 1923
A 1923 Ford owned by Morgan Trucking of Muscatine, Iowa. Note the tow bar used for hauling the truck, attached to its front axle. *American Truck Historical Society*

Chevrolet, 1924
Kron's Meat & Deli Shoppe of Woodlawn, Maryland, used this restored 1924 Chevrolet for promotional purposes. Note the radiator cap holder for small US flags for use in parades. *Chris and Pat Kron*

Chevrolet, 1924
Inside rear of the Kron's Chevrolet.
Chris and Pat Kron

Chevrolet, 1924
The uncluttered and uncomplicated
dashboard of the Kron's Chevrolet
harkens back to a simpler time.
Chris and Pat Kron

Chevrolet, 1924
The simple four-cylinder engine of the Kron's Chevrolet. *Chris and Pat Kron*

Ford Model AA, circa 1930
This Ford Model AA flatbed carried small signs advertising a restaurant and old-fashioned theater called "The Opry House." The personalized California license plates read, "OPRY HSE."

Ford, 1925
Central Freight Lines of Waco, Texas, used this 1925 Ford, which was similar to the one used by the firm's founder and current chairman, W. W. Callan, Sr., who was shown in the restored rig.

American LaFrance, circa 1925
Jack Daniel's Distillery often featured older trucks in its ads to promote a down-home feeling. Here was one of its public relations photos showing employees with a circa-1925 American LaFrance pumper. *Jack Daniel's*

Mack AB, 1925
A restored 1925 Mack AB used by South Side Carting of New Hyde Park, New York, for promotional purposes. *Albert Velocci*

Ford, 1926
Royal Trucking was the third owner of this 1926 Ford with a handcrank-lift dump body. Personalized California license plate read "TROYAL." *Roy Querio*

Blue Bird, 1927
The Blue Bird Body Company made school bus bodies, and here was its original first school bus body on a 1927 Ford chassis. In 1985, a US postage stamp was issued that showed a similar school bus. *Blue Bird Body Company*

REO, 1927
This 1927 Reo was one of the fleet of old trucks belonging to Cole's Express. *Coles Express*

Internationals, 1927 and 1975
A 1927 International parked next to a 1975 model; both were promoting Old Chicago beer. *Motor Vehicle Manufacturers Association*

Mack, 1927
Jones Motor Company of Spring City, Pennsylvania, restored this 1927 Mack tractor. Note the curved metal signs above each door.

Ford, 1927
Not a truck, but a 1927 Ford sedan outfitted with rail wheels and used for track inspection. In the center of the photo, Sam Y. Wilhite of the Columbus & Greenville Railway, presents the restored vehicle to the Smithsonian Institution in 1984. *Columbus & Greenville Railway*

Ford Model A, 1928
A 1928 Ford Model A panel that had been customized by lowering. It was fitted with a Ford V-6 engine and a Jaguar rear end. The sign on the side read, "W. T. Baldwin, Antiques." *Carl Unger*

Ford Model AA, 1928
Beverage Distributors, Inc., of Cleveland, Ohio, had this 1928 Ford Model AA restored. *J. A. Schwind*

Ford Model AA, 1928
This Ford Model AA was kept parked outside an antique store on the highway south of Carson City, Nevada. Wheels and frame were painted one color; fenders and lower body, a second color; and hood and cab, yet a third color.

Ford Model AA, 1928
Details of striping and lettering around the door of the Ford Model AA. *J. A. Schwind*

Ford Model AA, 1928
Details of striping and lettering at the rear of the Ford Model AA truck. *J. A. Schwind*

Mack, 1929
The owners of Holmes Transportation, Inc., of Framingham, Massachusetts, were able to track down their original 1929 Mack. They later restored it to as-new condition.

Fageol, 1929
A 1929 Fageol, which Gulf Oil purchased new and later reacquired for restoration. It's now used mainly in the Houston, Texas, area for service station grand openings. *Gulf Oil Products Co.*

162

White, 1929
A 1929 White, restored and used by a Volvo/White
dealer. *Volvo/White, New River Valley Truck Plant,
Dublin, Virginia*

Chapter 10

1930-1942 Vintage Commercial Trucks

This chapter covers a much shorter period of truck model years than do the other chapters; however, in terms of development of trucks and trucking this was probably the most significant decade or so. Trucks before 1930 were sometimes little more than motorized wagons. Their range of operations was short; they displaced and replaced the horse.

In terms of mechanical refinements and exterior appearance, the decade of the thirties was important to trucks. Some of the most attractive trucks ever produced are associated with that era. Auto and truck designs were similar; after World War II they would diverge. Intercity highways were paved and the trucking industry, as we know it today, developed.

Trucks from this era are attractive candidates for restoration because they can be safely operated on streets and highways. You will see more examples of customizing, or "hot rods," because it is possible to modify the performance of these vehicles.

Numerous pictures in this chapter show restored trucks at work in their advertising function, representing an exciting era for trucks and trucking.

Ford Model AA, circa 1930
A Ford Model AA dump truck used in a July 4 parade assembly area. It advertised the Barnyard Garage of Novato, California.

Ford Model AA, circa 1930
Roadway Express, one of the nation's largest motor carriers, used this Model AA Ford to celebrate its fiftieth anniversary in 1980. *Roadway Express, Inc.*

Chevrolet, 1930
Hays Old Truck Museum of Woodland, California, used this 1930 Chevrolet open-cab pickup.

Pierce-Arrow, 1930
A huge 1930 Pierce-Arrow dump truck, restored and used by Peter Scalamandre & Sons, a contractor.

Pierce-Arrow, 1930
A modern decal was added to the side door of the Scalamandre Pierce-Arrow.

Chevrolet, circa 1930
A circa-1930 Chevrolet used by a Canadian trucking firm. *Canada Transport Limited*

Divco, circa 1930s
Hood's Dairy of Boston had both an old Divco milk truck and a battery-powered, child's-size model.

Chevrolet, 1930
This Chevrolet fire engine from about 1930 featured gold lettering promoting a barbecue ribs restaurant. *Wayne Sorensen*

1932-1982

International, circa 1930s
Carolina Carriers used this picture on a colored holiday greetings card sent out in 1982.

Chevrolet, 1930
A restored 1930 Chevrolet with dump body, used by the General Body Company of Chicago. A newer Mack was in the rear. *General Body Co.*

Mack, 1931
A 1931 Mack bus from Greyhound's fleet of old buses.
Greyhound

Ford, 1932
This was a 1932 Ford B tractor, pulling a stake trailer, and used by Sullivan Contractors of Everitt, Massachusetts.

Maccar, 1933
The St. Johnsbury Trucking Company of Holliston, Massachusetts, restored this 1933 Maccar. *St. Johnsbury Trucking Company*

Ford, 1933
Ray Jason, a San Francisco Bay Area juggler, performs in parades on the bed of this moving 1933 Ford.

Ford, 1933
A 1933 unrestored Ford advertising a used auto parts shop. The lettering on the door read, "courtesy car."

Chevrolet, 1933
Strevel's Market of Spring Lake, Michigan, used this 1933 Chevrolet Canopy Express for promotional purposes. *Strevel's*

Buick, 1934, and GMC, 1949
Peter Pan Bus Lines, Inc., of Springfield, Massachusetts, restored a 1934 Buick sedan that was similar to the one first used when the company was founded. It featured a luggage rack on the roof. In the picture, it's on the left. Next to it was a 1949 GM bus, and to the right, part of a modern bus. *Peter Pan Bus Lines*

Chevrolet, 1934
A 1934 restored Chevrolet used by a San Francisco delicatessen.

International, 1934
Risberg's Truck Lines of Portland, Oregon, restored this 1934 International. *Risberg's*

Ford, 1934
A 1934 Ford tractor-trailer used by Churchill Truck Lines, a firm based in Missouri.

Dodge, 1934
A San Francisco antique store used this 1934 Dodge for deliveries. *Gary Alexander*

Pirsch, circa 1935
This mid-1930s Pirsch fire engine was used by the Urbana, Illinois, post of the American Legion in parades.

White, circa 1935
A restored Labatt's beer truck, with a mid-1930s White tractor. Picture was taken at EXPO 1986, in Vancouver, British Columbia.

Ford, 1936
Omar Electric of Franklin Park, Illinois, used this 1936 Ford half-ton panel.

Dodge, 1936

A 1936 Dodge restored by the *Hemmings Motor News* staff and modified mechanically so it could travel at highway speeds. This was one of three trucks of simi-lar age the magazine staff used for traveling to old car meets during the summer months. *Hemmings Motor News, photo copyright 1985, John Barber*

Ford, 1936
This 1936 Ford pickup was used by a Sun Valley, California, truck parts dealer.

Chevrolet, 1936
Sign on stake rack in this 1936 Chevrolet pickup read, "Tom Crooks Insurance." *Dorothy Crooks*

Ford, 1936
A 1936 Ford pickup, painted silver and parked in a resort area in northern California, used to advertise water jets.

IT'S NEVER TOO LATE TO REMANUFACTURE!

1936 WHITE

REMANUFACTURED IN 1986

ABC, 1936
ABC Bus Manufacturing, Inc., builds and rebuilds buses. The company restored a 1936 national park bus, which once ran in Glacier National Park. It is now featured in company ads. *ABC Bus Manufacturing*

Ford, 1937
A customized 1937 Ford panel used by an auto parts dealer.

White, 1937
A 1937 White national park bus, one of two owned by a firm that provided balloon rides.

Plymouth, 1937
A 1937 Plymouth pickup with twin sidemounts, used by a landscaping service. *Techniart*

Chevrolet, 1937
Macy Movers of Berkeley, California, purchased this Chevrolet new in 1937 and still runs it in local parades. *Macy Movers, Inc.*

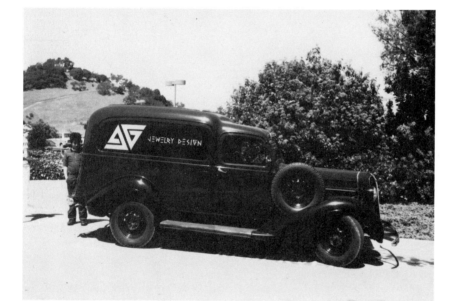

Dodge, circa 1938
A late 1930s Dodge, used by a jewelry vendor.

Kenworth, 1938
A 1938 Kenworth national park bus with an open top, now used by the Olivine Corporation.

Kenworth, 1938
Close-up of the left rear of the 1938 Kenworth national park bus showing the Olivine Corporation logo.

GMC, 1938
This was once a 1938 GMC hook-and-ladder truck. It now carries a sign and spotlight for use in celebrating grand openings. *W. M. Watts*

Chevrolet, 1939
A customized 1939 Chevrolet panel used by Sales Aids, Inc., a firm that promotes advertising novelties. *Mike Aigner*

Hudson, circa 1940s
This early 1940s Hudson pickup, with new wire wheels, was used by Classic City Automotive of Auburn, Indiana. *Bob Hovorka*

Ford, circa 1940
A Ford cab-over-engine, circa 1940, used by Dana Watson and Son, building movers, in Naples, Maine. *Dana E. Watson*

Ford, 1941
A restored and lowered 1941 Ford panel delivery used by Greer Enterprises.

180

White, 1941
Greer Trucking, of Beaver Falls, Pennsylvania, shows this 1941 White tractor-trailer combination.

Chevrolet, 1941
This 1941 Chevrolet panel was used to promote a Santa Cruz, California, restaurant.

Ford, 1941
A 1941 Ford light pickup used by a San Jose auto parts supplier.

Chevrolet, 1941
A 1941 Chevrolet sedan delivery with "Berkeley Warehouse and Drayage" painted on the side panel.

Ford, 1942
A 1942 Ford sedan delivery used by Goldenrod Garage.

Chapter 11

1946-1975 Vintage Commercial Trucks

When dealing with trucks built since World War II, the issue of "How old is old?" may be of concern. Many post-World War II trucks are still running around in relatively original shape, at least in parts of California and other states with warm climates where highways aren't salted. We're dealing with a time period where there's an overlap between restored old trucks and old trucks that have been well preserved.

From an advertising standpoint, choosing a postwar truck has two advantages. First, they can be operated safely under all traffic conditions. Second, they are young enough that they should have more appeal to mass markets.

The pictures in this chapter are of both restored trucks and trucks that have been very well maintained. Some remain in daily use!

Chevrolet, circa 1940s
A 1940s Chevrolet, still in use at weekend flea markets.

Peterbilt, circa 1940s
Opperman & Son of Healdsburg, California, restored this early Peterbilt lowbed from the 1940s. Note the company name on the panel above the rear wheels.

Freightliner, 1947

Consolidated Freightways (CF), one of the nation's largest motor carriers, restored this 1947 Freightliner. From about 1940 until 1981, CF owned Freightliner, building trucks for its own use and for sale to others. This truck, #162, started hauling for CF in the spring of 1947. In 1986, it was "discovered" in Merlin, Oregon, hauling lumber after it had passed through nine different owners and traveled an estimated 7 million miles. CF repurchased the truck in December 1986, and ten retired CF mechanics restored it. On October 1988, CF held a ceremony recognizing the ten workers and their restoration efforts. *Steve Slocum, Consolidated Freightways*

Dodge, 1946
A 1946 Dodge panel used by Santa Rosa Dodge.

International, 1947
Rechtien International Trucks of Miami, Florida, used this restored 1947 International for promotions.
Richard C. Rechtien

Ford, 1947
Scritch's Auto Restoration of Glendale, California, used this 1947 Ford sedan delivery as a shop car. *Dick Scritchfield*

Ford, 1948
A 1948 Ford pickup, whose owner still drives it daily. The wheels were not stock.

Federal, 1948
A restored 1948 Federal tractor-trailer combination. *Coles Express*

Dodge, 1948, Ford, 1952, and Chevrolet, 1964

Unrestored old trucks have a "funky" appearance and can also be used for promotional purposes. Here is a pictures of three trucks used to promote entertainment places that featured country music. The trucks, a 1948 Dodge, a 1952 Ford, and a 1964 Chevrolet all appeared in a recent Fourth of July parade in Marin County, California.

Chevrolet, 1948
Mid-State Sign Company of Murfreesboro, Tennessee, used this customized 1948 Chevrolet panel truck.

Peterbilt, 1948
A long-wheelbase 1948 Peterbilt tractor advertised a moving company's service.

Ford, 1949
This 1949 Ford stake truck appeared in a film about the Boston Brink's robbery. The sign on the side now advertises an old truck collectors' club.

Chevrolet, 1949
A 1949 Chevrolet tractor/trailer rig run by Harold Edwards, a stock and grain hauler from Omaha, Nebraska. *American Truck Historical Society*

GMC, 1949
G.A.P. Shippers Services of Los Angeles showed this 1954 GMC tractor.

GMC, 1950
A 1950 GMC pickup with camper body, parked in Tucson along a main road.

Freightliner, 1950
A restored 1950 Freightliner that the company donated to the Smithsonian Institution. *Freightliner*

Ford, circa 1950
Michael Davidson of Wilton, New Hampshire, ran a number of older trucks in his business. Here was a Ford, built in about 1950, rigged to carry and install septic tanks. *Michael Davidson*

Chevrolet, 1950
A restored 1950 Chevrolet sedan delivery advertising the Valley Bakery.

Mack, circa 1950s
A.N.D. Service of Carlstadt, New Jersey, ran a fleet of mid-fifties to mid-sixties Mack tow trucks. This picture of a mid-fifties Mack was copied from a printed colored picture that appearerd on the reverse side of the firm's business cards. *Steven P. Sass*

White, 1951
A 1951 White restored by Volvo/White in Dublin, Virginia. *Volvo/White*

Diamond-T, 1951
Jack Thompson restored this 1951 Diamond-T dump. The firm's name and phone number were on the door.

Pontiac, 1953
A 1953 Pontiac, once an ambulance, used by an auto sales company. *Kent Harkins*

Ford, 1953
George Kaiser of Collingdale, Pennsylvania, used this 1953 Ford wrecker.

Brockway, 1956
A restored 1956 Brockway. The sign on the door read, "Wm. Kramp, haulage." *Ron Kramp*

Chevrolet, 1956
This 1956 Chevrolet pickup was run by a firm that sold parts for 1955–1959 Chevrolets.

GMC, circa 1957
A well-maintained late-fifties GMC with a dump body, carrying an election sign and parked near an intersection.

Ford Ranchero, 1957

A heavily customized 1957 Ford Ranchero, operated by an auto upholstery shop in Tacoma, Washington. Some of the custom work included chopping the roof height 3in, front fenders extended 2in, and rear fenders extended 6in with 1964 Ford taillights tunneled 6in. The front fenders were tucked with a handmade roll pan. A roll pan from a 1953 Studebaker was used at the rear. A scooped 1958 Ford hood was used, as was 1958 Ford side chrome. The door handles and emblems were shaved. The interior was upholstered using black vinyl and gold velvet. *Bob Jasper*

Previous page
Mack, 1961
Matlack, Inc., a well-known hauler of industrial chemicals, restored this 1961 Mack tractor and 1946 Heil trailer to help commemorate the firm's 100th anniversary in 1988. The rig toured the country, visiting terminals and customers. *Matlack, Inc.*

Volkswagen, circa 1960s
This VW tow truck was nicknamed "Short Stroke," and its GVW (gross vehicle weight) was 26,000 ounces, with the "oz" in the smallest of lettering.

Grumman, circa 1960s
An old Grumman step-van, probably on a Chevrolet chassis, parked adjacent to a highway and used to carry advertisements.

Chevrolet, circa 1960s
An early 1960s Chevrolet pickup carrying a roofer's sample roofs parked permanently alongside the road in central Wisconsin.

Chevrolet, El Camino, circa 1967
A well-maintained Chevrolet El Camino from the late 1960s used by a custom auto shop.

GMC Sprint, circa 1975
A mid-seventies GMC Sprint used by a New Hampshire truck dealer.

Chapter 12

Restoring and Painting Commercial Trucks

Once you accept the challenge of restoring an old truck or bus for use as advertising, you must consider many factors. At the risk of appearing to lack focus, this chapter will list and discuss many of the factors one should take into account without pointing to a single conclusion.

Not mentioned at any length here, but very important, is cost of restoration. This varies widely, and much depends on the quality and completeness of whatever rig you are considering for restoration.

This picture illustrates the separation between a truck's chassis and body. This was an old photo and shows a laundry body on sawhorses. Some truck bodies were switched from an old chassis to a new one, although this didn't happen often as the body typically wore out along with the truck and because, over the years, the dimensions of truck chassis changed. *Crown Coach*

This and several other pictures show details of the restoration of a World War I-vintage International, performed by Winross Restorations of Palmyra, New York. Here we see a worker examining the numerous detailed photos taken before and during dismantling. *Winross Restorations*

Choosing the Vintage of Truck

Trucks from before 1930 tend to be slow and probably cannot be driven on modern highways. They can be driven only locally and trailered to more distant points.

Trucks from the 1930s, especially the late thirties, can be operated at highway speed, were fitted with hydraulic brakes, and can be converted to 12volt operation. They usually do not need to be trailered to events.

Post-World War II trucks are near modern in many respects and can be restored and outfitted to be operated on the highway. Parts are easier to locate since many of these trucks are still in day-to-day service and covered by conventional motor vehicle insurance.

If your firm has owned an old vehicle since it was new, it is the most likely candidate for restoration. There is additional advertising value in being able to use one's own truck; and more than one firm has kept (or managed to track down and buy back) "old number one." Another

good option is to buy and restore a truck similar to "old number one." It is also a good idea to use a truck of a vintage similar to that of the firm it was selected to advertise. A slogan such as "1922 Graham Bros.— made the year we were founded" might be painted on a restored truck's side.

You should also consider the age of the market you are attempting to attract or interest. Today's "young" people, for example, may view a Ford Model T as a relatively uninteresting relic of some long bygone era, while they might be very interested in a truck from the 1950s, or even 1960s. (One of the most popular courses on many college campuses these days deals with the 1960s!) My own theory is that people interested in old autos and trucks are most interested in those which were on the streets at about the time they first obtained a driver's license.

George Humphrey, from Poland Springs, Maine, is well known in truck history groups because of his several nicely restored rigs. Writing in the *Wheels of Time* (September/ October 1983) about choosing a truck to restore, he said: "It might be something you admired as a child or a truck your father or grandfather owned. When I was 10 years old in the late thirties, I saw the big Bulldog Macks working on highway projects and hauling lowbeds. I was always more interested in the big trucks than the small ones. Even though my dad worked for International Harvester Company and I drove a KR11 International as a young man of 19, I fell in love with the Bulldog. Naturally my first truck restoration was a 1922 Mack AC."

Note the details of the original hood, which must be repaired. The word "International" was barely visible in raised lettering. *Winross Restorations*

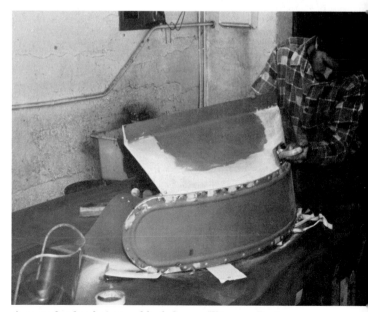

A new fender being rubbed down. *Winross Restorations*

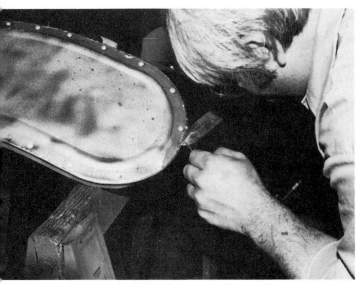

Solder was applied to cracks by hand, a painstaking operation. *Winross Restorations*

In any event, if you are restoring a truck for advertising purposes, and the choice of vintage is open, you should give some thought to the ages of those you wish to reach, rather than the vintage of truck that most interests you.

Choosing a Make of Truck

As for make of truck, you have many choices, although the number of different makes shrinks

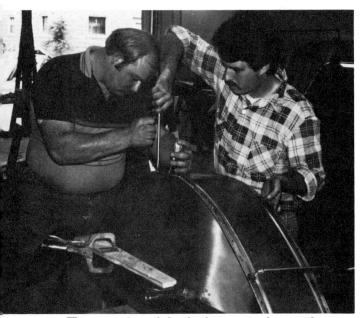

The mounting of the fender required more than one pair of hands. *Winross Restorations*

as you move to later time periods. Over 1,000 different makes of trucks have been built in the United States. In addition, almost every early auto was available with either a pickup box or delivery body. By 1940, the number of makes had shrunk to about twenty-five, and today the figure is about half of that (although many imports are available). You could choose a make associated with the early days of your firm, or you could choose a "regional" make of truck, that is, one that had been manufactured in or near the area where the restored truck is likely to be displayed. Following are a few examples of regional trucks and their place and time span of manufacture: Brockway (Cortland, New York) 1912-1977; Corbitt (Henderson, North Carolina) 1913-1958; Fageol (Oakland, California) 1916-1939; Hug (Highland, Illinois) 1922-1942; Moreland (Burbank, California) 1911-1941; Schacht (Cincinnati, Ohio) 1910-1938; Sterling (Milwaukee, Wisconsin) 1916-1953; and Stewart (Buffalo, New York) 1912-1941.

If you want to learn what is "popular" or what is "rare," The American Truck Historical Society has a registry of trucks twenty-five years or more years old. While not complete by any means, the numbers are certainly indicative of the relative numbers of the older trucks. Fords make up about one-quarter of the vehicles listed. They and six other makes (Chevrolet, Dodge, GMC, International, Mack, and White) account for nearly three-quarters of the old trucks. Most old trucks fall into one of two categories: popular or rare. Fords are especially popular. Examples of "rare" makes are those such as Alco, Biederman, Chase, Defiance, and Eagle. Very rare trucks such as these might be real challenges to restore.

If you can use an old fire engine or truck in promoting your business, you should be able to find one fairly easily, since fire departments retire nearly all of their apparatus as it reaches the age of about thirty years. Fire apparatus is usually in good shape because it has been garaged its entire life; has few miles on the odometer, and there are active groups of collectors and restorers. It is expensive to repair and to store, however. Chicago radio station WFYR uses the "fire" theme and owns an 1920s Seagrave pumper that it displays in its marketing area. In the San Francisco area, several taverns have old fire engines with the tavern's name painted in gilt. They are used in parades, usually to carry ragtime bands. John Gunnell, of Krause Publications, writing in the March/April 1987 issue of *Double Clutch*, said:

"With fire trucks. . . , restoring such vehicles to mint condition is very expensive because of their size and intricacy. As a result, many collec-

Ford Model T autos could be converted easily to trucks. Here, a circa-1915 sedan has its rear body sitting on the ground while its owner reattached the license and rear lantern after installing the pickup box. A person restoring this chassis today could justifiably end up with either an auto or a truck. *Weber's, Fort Worth*

When restoring trucks, it's difficult to deterine what was and what was not "authentic." This old photo shows a handsome, enclosed cargo box being built on the rear of an unidentified automobile, which had right-hand steering. *Special Collections, University of Arizona Library*

tors will limit repairs to these...vehicles to a 'shade tree' restoration entailing only basic fix-ups and a quick coat of paint. They tend to be used more for fun driving than winning trophies at a show."

Roy Ames wrote an article entitled "Pickups Worth Collecting" in the October 1980 issue of *Special-Interest Autos*. He recommended the following:

American Bantam (1930s)—small, 1/4ton capacity trucks.

Chevrolet Cameo (mid-1950s)—highly styled pickups.

Corvair Loadside & Rampside (early 1960s)—this was the truck version of the auto; some loaded through a ramp on the right side.

Crosley (1939–1952)—tiny U.S. built vehicles.

Diamond-T (1930s)—extremely attractive truck.

Ford Model A (1928–1931)—very popular.

Ford Falcon Ranchero (early 1960s)—during this period, Ford offered its Ranchero on the small Falcon chassis.

Goodyear restored the Wingfoot Express; here's the 1917 Packard truck as found and before restoration, resting in a Minnesota bog where it had been abandoned over forty years earlier. *Goodyear*

Hudson (1929–1948)—pickup versions of the auto.

Mack, Jr. (1936–1938)—built by Reo for Mack so that Mack would have a light truck for its dealers to market.

Morris Minor—a small vehicle, made in England.

Plymouth (1937–1941)—similar to Dodge trucks; in addition there were sedan deliveries on the passenger car chassis.

Powell (1955–1956)—assembled out of old Plymouth parts with fiberglass styling.

Willys (prewar)—Willys built an auto that was smaller than typical autos of the late thirties; it also offered light truck models.

Most evidence suggests that one of the popular makes, and not too old, is probably the easiest choice for restoration. If you do choose an older, less well-known model and make, you should do so only after some careful analysis. Mention should also be made of "parts" trucks. If you are restoring an uncommon make and model of truck, it is often advisable to buy a second, nearly identical, model and "cannibalize" it for parts. Indeed, and with luck, you may find all the parts needed for a restoration this way. This is usually cheaper than buying parts on a piece-by-piece basis.

Choosing a Truck Body Style

As for body style of truck, pickups were—and are—the most common. Their only disadvantage is that they are not enclosed, a problem for the user who wants to carry promotional materials. For some businesses, the body style would be that used in the trade, for example, bottler's, plate-glass, refrigerated, or tow-truck bodies. Only common body styles—pickup, panel, and stake—were, and are, built by the truck chassis

The completed body being loaded on a trailer and about to be moved to where it would be placed on the Packard's chassis. *Goodyear*

manufacturers. Other bodies are built and attached to the frame by specialized truck body builders. Truck trailers are built by firms other than the manufacturer of trucks.

Size is also related to your choice of body or trailer style. Larger trucks and truck-trailer rigs are more impressive in an advertising sense, but they are also more expensive to restore and to garage when not in use.

A much wider range of individual truck body styles exists than most would imagine. The following list of available bodies from the mid-1950s is taken from a Chevrolet Truck *Silver Book* (a catalog of parts, bodies, and other equipment made by others to fit Chevrolet chassis, and marketed through Chevrolet truck dealers): "A" frame glass-carrying, acid tanks, air com-

A new body being built for the Wingfoot Express. *Goodyear*

Adding the final touches to the Wingfoot Express's ten-month restoration job. Price tag for total job was in the neighborhood of $100,000. *Goodyear*

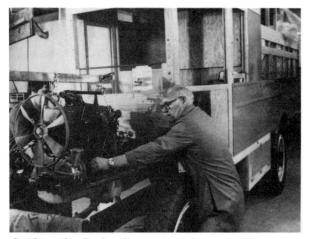

Guiding the Packard's restored four-cylinder engine into place. *Goodyear*

pressors, airport buses, airport crash, ambulance, armored car, asphalt tank, bakery, beer, beverage, bookmobiles, bottlers, brick-loading/unloading, bulk cement, bus, cable splicers, canopy, cargo van, cattle rack, cement mixer, chest X-ray, cleaners and dyers, clinic (mobile), coal, concrete, contractors, dairy, delivery, dental clinic, department store, dry freight, dump, electric meter installer's, express, farm, feed, fertilizer spreading, fire-fighting, florists, food products, frozen foods, fuel oil, funeral coach, furniture, garbage, gas cylinder, gas line construction, gas meter installation, gasoline transport, grain, grocers', hearses, high-lift, horse vans, ice-control spreader, ice, ice cream, insulated, laundry, limestone spreader, livestock, logging, lumber, machine shop, meat packers,

milk delivery, oil field equipment, open-top, painters', pallet-loading, parcel delivery, pick-up, pie distributors', plant protection, platform, plumbers', police patrol, produce, public utility service, radio units, refrigerator, rescue crew, road-building, school bus, self-unloading, squad car, stake, station wagon, street flusher, street light maintenance, taxi, telephone installation, tree trimmer, and wrecker.

The list of trailers is about half as long, and contains trailers built for similar purposes. In addition, there are some specialized trailers, such as for carrying poles.

We asked a number of truck restoration shops which body style they would recommend for restoration. Their answers were:

• Panel because it had more ad space on sides and rear.

• Pickups are the most popular, but size must be a consideration.

• Body styles that have a significance to the locale of the parades.

• Pickups—least cost to restore.

• 1-ton, 1½-ton, or 2-ton; heavier truck is more distinctive.

• Panels can carry promotional materials inside.

They also indicated that it was easier to find parts for pickups than for any other truck body style.

Restoration Costs

Individuals who had restored old trucks indicated a wide range of costs, sometimes climing into the tens of thousands of dollars. Several indicated that the potential restorer seek advice from the restoration shop before buying and old truck to restore

While these are large outlays of money, they might not be unreasonable in the context of a

When the rear-axle differential from the old truck was removed, it was discovered that it lacked the great gear ring. Luckily, one was obtained from a Packard truck buff. *Goodyear*

The Wingfoot Express's restored chassis fitted with the leaf-spring suspension. *Goodyear*

firm's advertising budget. Most other forms of advertising are also expensive.

An alternative is for the truck owner to do part or all of the work him- or herself. That will save cash, but take time, and provide an interesting—and sometimes frustrating—hobby. If are planning on writing off the truck restoration as a business advertising expense, this might also be a good time to discuss the entire idea with your tax accountant. In any event, it is useful to explore the possibility of doing the restoration yourself; this will help you choose a better truck and will help in dealing with professional restoration services. Another useful early step is

About fifteen years ago, Freightliner Corporation restored one of the first trucks it manufactured, and then donated it to the Smithsonian Institution. Here, some Freightliner employees—including some who worked on the original truck in 1950—are shown working on the cab restoration. *Freightliner*

to find some original truck and truck body literature, paint charts, and so on for the rig to be
restored.

We also asked restoration shops what types
of problems they encountered because the vehicle
was a truck (rather than an auto) and whether
trucks were easier or more difficult to restore
than autos. Answers were:

• Twice as expensive and half the value! You
have basically two bodies to do rather than one
as with a passenger car. Trucks are more difficult to restore since they usually are in a more
run-down condition.

• Height, weight, and length. Difficult to
move around the shop; scaffolds are necessary in
some cases.

• The bodies just take up more space in the
shop. Trucks are more difficult to restore because
parts unique to trucks aren't as available. Usually, trucks are more worn out than cars.

• Finding original parts is difficult because
of their lesser numbers. I find trucks to be more
time-consuming when it comes to the drivetrain.

• More difficult because of their worn-out
condition. Few were ever kept in garages.

• Sometimes body sheet metal and trim only
fits trucks and is very hard to find.

• Trucks are a little easier to do, but not
much. The cargo box is sometimes a problem
because of lack of parts.

• More difficult to restore. Harder to find
parts except for Fords and Chevrolets.

• Restoration of a truck up to 2 tons in size is
comparable to restoring an auto.

Generally, trucks are cheaper to restore than
cars because of glass, upholstery, instrumenta-
tion, and other appointments. Show requirements are less stringent.

In the restoration of automobiles, especially
"classics" (old Packards, Pierce-Arrows, and so

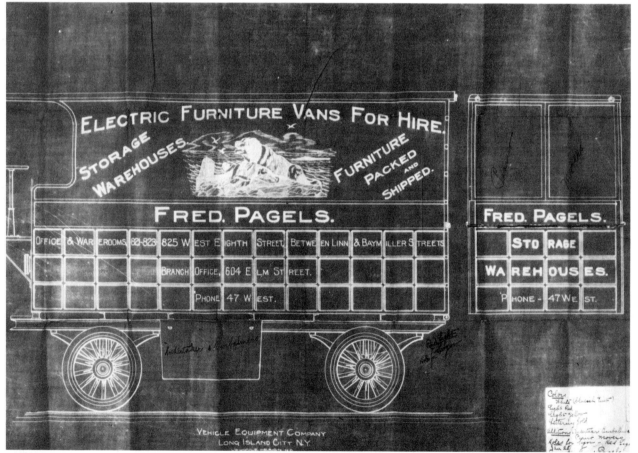

A 1906 signpainter's drawing for decorating an electric
van. It was necessary to space the lettering between
the wooden strips along the side of the body. In dark
ink were added the words: "Undertakers and
Embalmers," which would go on the battery box
between the wheels; the words "Piano Movers," which

would go on the tops of the rear doors; and some
instructions for attaching the red taillamp. A note in
the lower right corner read, "Colors: White (bluish
tint), light red, light yellow, lettering gold." The original drawing was to the scale of 1in equals 1ft. *Allied
Van Lines, Chicago*

on), it is considered extremely important that the car be restored to exactly the way it was originally manufactured or outfitted. When cars such as this are shown in competitions, they lose points for every deviation from original condition. Standards for displaying restored old trucks are much less stringent. At old truck shows awards are usually given to the oldest, the longest truck and trailer, the one that traveled the longest distance to the show, and so on. These less exacting standards are used for a number of reasons. Three are historical:

1. Trucks model years are often more difficult to ascertain. Some models have been in production for as long as twenty years and the truck manufacturers would modify their product only in response to large orders and then might or might not revert back to the style and equipment they'd formerly been turning out.

2. In states where the truck's registration fees were based on its age, with older trucks being taxed less as the truck wore out, the original owner would gradually replace everything except the serial number plate.

3. Truck owners and truck body shops always feel they have wide latitude in modifying the truck from time to time as is necessary to meet their needs.

The last reason illustrates the attitudes and temperaments of people currently interested in old trucks. They prefer to keep it as more of a "fun" activity and not have competitions that are decided, in fact, on the amounts of money various competitors have spent in their respective quests for "perfect" restorations. Hence, the old truck restorer can feel safe in deviating from the original as he or she undertakes the restoration. Two suggestions will be made, however. One is to alter the outward appearance of the truck as little as possible. The second is to give some thought before making irreversible changes. (The day may come when you will want a more authentic restoration.)

A portion of a sketch that appeared in the late 1930s in *The Automobile Trimmer and Painter*. It shows how curved lines and slanted lettering can have a streamlining effect. *Harrah's Automobile Collection, Reno*

A number of modifications can be made to an old truck. Some are almost a necessity if it is to be driven in modern-day traffic. They include adding turn signals and side mirrors. Sealed beam headlight units are available for late 1930s models that look almost like the original lights. If the wiring must be replaced, it might be wise to move to a 12-volt system. For trucks that are to be driven a lot, the entire power train should possibly be changed. A more recent and more powerful engine might be installed and the gear ratios changed. For example, in Goodyear's 1917 Packard Wingfoot Express restoration, the drivetrain was modified to increase the truck's top speed from 25mph to 40mph. All old trucks should carry a fire extinguisher, mounted in brackets. *Hemmings Motor News* has several late 1930s panels that have been modified some to accompany highway endurance runs by adding three-point seatbelts, a racing-type fuel cell, and an earphone system that allowed the driver and passengers to talk with each other above the roar of the truck's engine and wind. For many post-World War II Chevrolet and Ford models, it's possible to buy power steering, air conditioning units, and AM/FM radios.

Finding Restoration Parts

Much has been said so far about the availability of parts. For Fords and Chevrolets, it's easy to buy parts. The market is so large that firms manufacture new parts that are identical to original equipment. (It's apparently possible to build a complete Ford Model A out of these newly manufactured parts!) Also, a number of manuals deal with the restoration of these popular makes. For a beginning "do-it-yourselfer" a Ford, Chevrolet, or Dodge would be the truck to start with.

Many truck parts are interchangeable. This is true for trucks of the same make but different model years, and also "related" makes such as Dodge and Plymouth, or Chevrolet and GMC.

Drawing from the Pittsburgh Plate Glass Company's circa-1940 fleet painting manual. Drawing was of an International truck. *PPG Industries*

PAINTING CHART
For Pittsburgh Plate Glass Company Vehicles

The lettering shown on these reproductions indicates *position only.* For size, style and color—see reverse side.

Type A

Type B

Type D

Type C

Type E

A portion of a fleet painting chart used by Pittsburgh Plate Glass Company to ensure that all vehicles in its fleet had uniform appearance. This was pre-World War I; some vehicles were horse-drawn. *PPG Industries*

Many larger trucks, built before World War II, were referred to as "assembled" trucks, meaning that the manufacturer bought all the various parts and components he needed from outside suppliers and then assembled his make of truck, using his own grille, emblems, and a few other identifying marks to make his truck slightly different from the competition's. In the case of "assembled" trucks, there is a wide range of parts interchangeability. With some searching, you can find lists of which components were common to a number of different makes and models of trucks.

For light trucks there is also interchangeability with parts for autos of the same make and vintage. This would hold for just about anything except parts unique to the truck body. There was even some interchangeability between parts used on trucks and autos of different makes. Take, for example, the sleek parking lamps that were mounted on the fender tops of 1936-41 Diamond-T trucks. Bob Flock, a noted Diamond-T restorer, in an article about these parking lights in the newsletter for Diamond-T restorers, said, in part:

"The teardrop-shaped fender mount parking lights...were furnished to Diamond-T by the Guide Division of General Motors. The lamps featured an inside-fluted milk glass lens, and chrome-plated bevel ring horizontally encircling

on your well-painted truck can be compared to a simil

This handsome job done in Kem Enamel Medium Yellow and Kem Enamel Vermili Art work done in S-W Quick-Drying Colors and finished with Kem Clear. Body Kelly Auto Body Co., Cincinnati. Trailer by the Lapeer-Trailmobile Co., Cincinnati. Pain and finished by O. H. Roth & Co., Cincinnati.

The caption under this Coca-Cola truck read, "This handsome job done in Kem Enamel Vermilion. Art work done in S-W Quick-Drying Colors and finished with Kem Clear." *Sherwin-Williams*

the lamp.... The parking lamp...was [also] offered by General Motors as an option accessory on the 1937-39 Chevrolet [autos].

"The extra cost of the parking lamp option is listed at $6.00 per pair in my [Flock's] 1937 Diamond-T factory sales brochure.... These original parking lamps are rare today, with prices in the several hundred dollar price range seen at swap meets! Chevy restorers and street rodders have driven the price up on these scarce accessories. Fortunately for those Diamond-T truckers without original accessory parking lamps, a company in southern California has begun reproducing them...[that firm] offers a very nice metal reproduction at a price of $79.00 per pair. The only variations from the original are a 12-volt bulb, frosted lens instead of milk glass, and lack of an inner catch at the rear of the top cover."

e Vance Storage and Transfer Co., Altoona, Pa., secured an unusually handsome effect selecting Kem Enamel in Brewster Green for this equipment, painted by O. H. Roth Co., d built by Kelly on Trailmobile chassis.

Sherwin-Williams provide a painting system to suit your op production methods without installation of special

These pictures appeared in a 1934 booklet put out by Sherwin-Williams and they're reproduced here because the original captions happened to describe the colors. This Mack double trailer was painted with Kem Enamel in Brewster Green. *Sherwin-Williams*

The body on this Railway Express electric was painted Kem Enamel Medium Green, and the chassis was Kem Enamel Vermilion. *Sherwin-Williams*

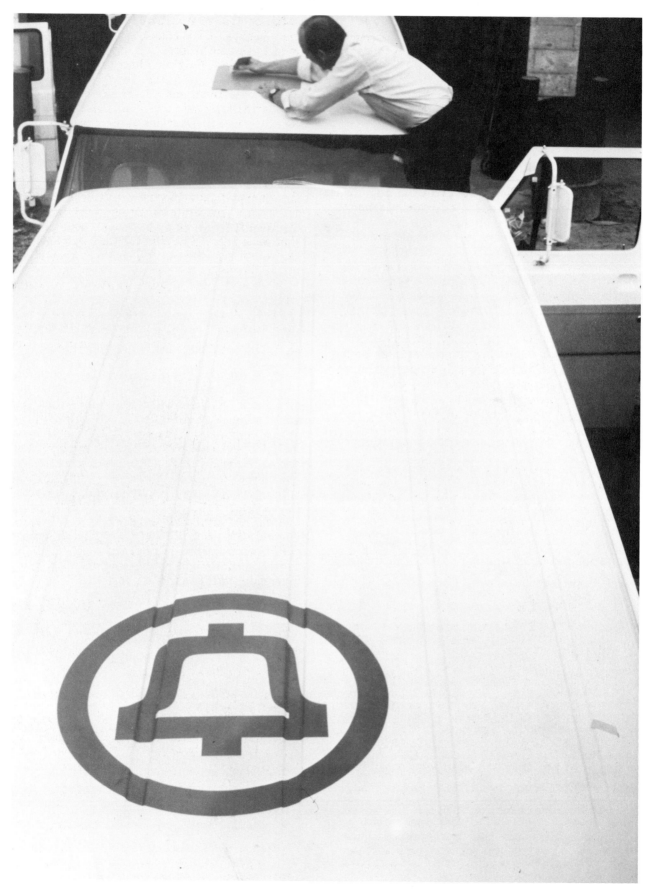

Previous page
One of the largest truck fleets in the country belonged to the Bell System. In the late 1960s, Bell changed from grey-olive-green to the grey-green, white, blue, and ochre we see today; one reason given for the white tops was that they reflect heat. This 1969 photo shows a worker applying a new seal decal to the roof of a Bell truck. *AT&T Photo Center*

Body Restoration

One unique segment of old truck restoration regards the body. Often, the firms that built

The paper mask stencils that were made available. The small drawing in the center shows how to cut and bend the vertical stroke on the "F" to fit the roof contour. Another sheet showed how to apply them and how to spray paint over them. *Arco*

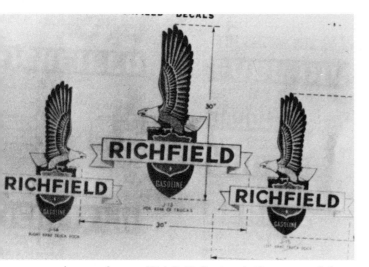

A page from a Richfield fleet painting manual from about 1950 showing the three decals that were available, one for each side door, and a larger one for the rear of the tank. *Arco*

truck bodies were entirely different from the manufacturer of the chassis. Some of these firms were little-known local blacksmiths or one-time wagon builders. Original plans and drawings are all but impossible to find. Initially, most truck bodies were made entirely of wood. Roofs were covered with coated fabrics to keep them watertight. Continual vibrations of operating on rough roads caused wooden joints to come apart; soon, thin sheets of metal were used to cover the wooden framework. Eventually, all-metal construction was used. For the restorer, there are even less rigorous "standards" for authenticity of the body restoration than there are for the truck chassis.

Several firms currently build wooden bodies that can be placed on small Ford, Chevrolet, and Dodge chassis from the 1920s. These body styles include express, pie wagon, pickup, and huckster. These firms also build open and closed wooden cabs.

For restoring some truck bodies, one would need access to a machine shop. "High-lift," dump, garbage, and wrecker bodies, for example, were

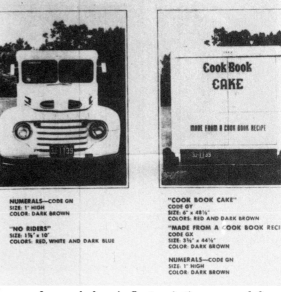

A page from a bakery's fleet-painting manual from about 1950. *American Bakeries Company*

The Monterey-Salinas Transit agency restored a 1947 Fageol Twin Coach bus, similar to the ones first operated in its service area. The firm found the bus model they wanted in Bremerton, Washington. *Monterey-Salinas Transit*

In starting the restoration of the Fageol, the finish was stripped down to bare metal. *Monterey-Salinas Transit*

made almost entirely of metal and metal parts and operated through mechanical or hydraulic means.

Painting Your Truck

Since you will probably use your restored truck for advertising purposes, choice of color and trim is extremely important. When looking through the pictures in this book for ideas, keep in mind that although the early pictures are in black and white and you are left to guess the colors, you may be able to find "old-timers" who remember what the original colors were. Old magazines from the 1930s contained color advertising; these ads might show how trucks used in some nationwide fleets were painted. Original truck sales literature and paint chips can also be obtained. Several paint companies also make an effort to aid auto restoration efforts.

Remember that truck restorations need not be perfectly authentic; the restorer has some latitude in choice of finish and color. Restorer George Humphrey said, "I would not recommend painting a large antique truck with lacquer

paint. Temperature changes and vibrations will crack and check it. I use modern enamel."

In addition to attempting to determine an early truck's color, you should look into the style of lettering that was originally applied. With luck, you can find an old photo or two in the firm's files or in the albums of former employees. Local historical societies often have large collections of old photos. They may also have old city Yellow Pages containing pictures of firms' delivery trucks, or at least their advertising slogans and logos.

The development of auto and truck painting is of some interest in itself, and you may be surprised to learn that, before quick-drying finishes, painting was the most time-consuming operation in the completion of an auto or truck. When more than one color was applied, the painter had to wait for each one to dry before starting with another.

The efforts of large firms to ensure that all trucks throughout their fleets were uniformly painted in order to reinforce the advertising message is called fleet graphics. Applying fleet

Here is the Fageol with its new colors and lettering applied. *Monterey-Salinas Transit*

graphics to any single restoration project is somewhat limited today, since modern finishes are recommended and many of the original "fleetwide" marking materials, such as decals or stencils, no longer exist.

Truck painting did not start with trucks. It was a carry-over from the painting of horse-drawn vehicles, which were made of wood. Early finishes, varnishes, and paints were neither long-lasting nor accommodating to the shrinkage of the wood and the cracks that resulted from vibrations of vehicular motion. Painters eventually overcame these problems by using pumice stone, which would rub down the putty, primers, and undercoatings of paint into a smooth foundation for the decorative layers. Metal hardware was usually finished separately.

Carriage (and early truck) painters also took a step in the direction of art by painting scrolls, stripes, monograms, crests, landscapes, and other scenes on nearly every available surface. That art form exists today on fire apparatus; some are still sold with extensive gold lettering and trim.

Early autos and trucks were finished in the same manner as carriages, but the finishes did not hold up, mainly because the autos and trucks received rougher treatment and exposure than the horse-drawn vehicles had. Engine heat blistered nearby paints, and they would peel. Various paints and varnishes were used, and anywhere from two to four weeks was required for the application, drying, and rubbing down of several coats. In damp weather, many vacant lots in Detroit would be crowded with new cars somewhere along in their painting cycle. Black enamel was the commonly used finish on Ford, Dodge, Overland, and GM products until the mid-twenties, according to Alfred P. Sloan, in his book, *My Years With General Motors*. Sloan went on to describe the development of Duco by DuPont scientists and GM technicians. Duco was both fast-drying and could carry bright pigment colors in suspension. Thus modern auto and truck finishing, as we know it today, was born.

Trucks usually went through at least two painting processes, and still do. First the chassis and cab were painted at the chassis manufacturer's plant; then the completed rig was painted after the body was attached. At this point, stripes and gold leaf lettering would be applied.

Here is the Fageol with its windows masked prior to painting. *Monterey-Salinas Transit*

(The gold leaf would be varnished over to protect it.) An article in a 1925 issue of *The Automobile Trimmer and Painter,* entitled "The Possibilities in Color for Truck Advertising," contained a number of points that would be valid to today's restorer. The initial concern was whether the user was in a trade where trucks were washed regularly; if not, dark colors were recommended. An example was given of coal trucks painted black with gold lettering, the choice of gold conveying the suggestions of glowing coals. Laundries, bake shops, confectioners, and grocers were advised to use white or other light colors (and to keep their trucks washed!). Produce vendors' trucks were to be painted shades of garden green. Trucks used by tea and coffee companies were to be painted the same bright colors as their retail packages.

Harmony with the owner's line of merchandise, combined with the maximum ability to command attention and permanently impress the spectator. This is the goal for which the painter should work. What are the most striking colors? Red, of course; orange, yellow and blue, following in the order named. In a way of speaking, red,

orange, and yellow are "dangerous" colors. Always the painter should keep in mind the customer's particular clientele.

For stores with products aimed at a higher class customer, the article recommended truck "colors suggestive of the mellow, soulful, restful, qualities.... Blue, purple, violet—those command attention."

The last step in painting the truck was the addition of hand lettering and striping. Then, as always, imagination was a useful tool to the truck painter who was trying to find more work. An article in a 1930 issue of *The Automobile Trimmer and Painter* entitled "How to Develop Profitable Commercial Fleet Business" gave these examples of how some jobs had been obtained by enterprising auto painters:

"In San Francisco a certain printing house makes a specialty of color work. The concern was approached by an automobile painter who suggested that its delivery truck could be used as a fitting advertisement for this specialty. He devised a color scheme, splashes of color in modernistic manner and landed the order.

"Another San Francisco establishment spe-

The fine finishing work of detailed trimming was done with a narrow brush. *Monterey-Salinas Transit*

cializes in the manufacture of window blinds. An automobile painter was approached with the request that he work out some idea whereby the delivery trucks operated by that concern should advertise the service in a highly attractive manner. The painter designed a color scheme in black and white. One half of the body was painted black, the other half white. In a conspicuous place on each side of the body the following was lettered in: 'A blind man drives this truck.'"

Many truck owners had more than one truck and wished to have them painted in a uniform manner. This uniformity was achieved in a number of ways. One was by fleet painting charts, which, in a sense, were very detailed instructions. Within the same shop, patterns were drawn on heavy paper, which was then laid flat on a soft, even surface. A small pinwheel device was then rolled along the lines, leaving a pattern of perforations along each line. This pattern was then taped on the side of the truck and dusted with chalk. A pattern of dots would mark the various lines to be followed by the painter. This pattern could be saved, and reused.

Another way to achieve uniformity was to prepare baked enamel aluminum sign panels and attach them to the truck. This had several advantages. The first was that truck "down-time" was reduced because the truck would be tied up only long enough to rivet on the completed sign. Through silkscreen processes any number of sign panels could be prepared and even shipped to different cities.

A variation of this, found mainly on newspaper trucks, was a metal frame enclosing a poster that would be changed every week or so. Mail, REA Express, and some telephone trucks also carried changeable posters.

A final development, and one still in use today, was the application of decalcomania transfers. These would be designed for each customer's needs and printed in batches. Before application there would be two layers to the sheet: the decal and its backing. The sheet would be applied to a clean surface on the truck, and the backing removed, leaving the decal in place. All sorts of pictures, symbols, and letters could be printed on decal transfers, and in more detail than could be accomplished by the sign painter. The sign painter was still needed for providing local information, such as the firm's phone number. However, the decals, which required little skill to apply, displaced many sign painters from their jobs. (It was also possible to order "custom" decal transfers for single jobs; the decal transfer printer had the ability to produce small or single orders. And standard letterings or symbols could be sold to different customers, possibly only the using firm's name would be different.)

If a restorer is lucky enough to find fleet painting charts or manuals that cover the old truck he or she is restoring, then almost no questions will be left unanswered. The charts or manuals varied in form and length. Another example of a fleet-painting manual found in the ARCO files from about 1950 was eighteen pages long and dealt with the painting of "Richfield" petroleum trucks. The instructions covered both the painting of new trucks as well as the repainting of old trucks to conform with the new coloring scheme. (On older trucks, for example, chrome

Note the chrome details on the top front corners of the Fageol bus, as well as the nameplate. *Monterey-Salinas Transit*

218

was to be carefully inspected and—if in poor shape—sanded and painted.)

Lettering instructions included some requirements to meet the company's internal needs, such as painting the capacity of each tank. Also, various state requirements for lettering were listed. These included an indication of the vehicle's weight and the size and placement of the words "gasoline" or "fuel oil" for whatever inflammable product was being carried.

There was a two-page chart listing the quantities needed of colored paints, primers, surfacers, and stencil adhesive, by size of truck. Two of the colors, "Richfield Blue" and "Richfield Yellow" had to be obtained from the company. Other materials could be obtained from Fuller paint dealers. Decals showing the Richfield eagle could be obtained from the company, as could stencil masks needed for truck lettering. Because of the different truck sizes involved, it was necessary to have differing instructions for each size class.

Numerous pages were devoted to showing three views—front, rear, and side—of each style and size of truck to be painted. Finally, a sheet described how to obtain bids from local paint shops. The bidder had to specify that he would "furnish all labor, equipment and materials necessary (except stenciling masks, decals, and blue and yellow paint) to steam clean, paint and letter in Richfield colors in accordance with Richfield painting specifications...."

A newer fleet painting manual, dating from the early 1970s from the Bell System, contains instructions for painting and repainting trucks with the Bell System's new four-color scheme. The sixty-eight-page manual is printed in full color and even has two pages devoted to handcarts, lift trucks, and compressor-trailers. Phone company trucks also used to carry posters, but when the new, four-color scheme was introduced, the manual said:

"Many system companies have been using advertising posters on their vehicles. With the introduction of our new corporate graphics, this policy has been changed.

"The new Bell System vehicles are a bright two-tone design with strong identification for the System company. So, it is important that these graphics are not obscured, cluttered or complicated by advertising posters that are a secondary form of communication.

"Therefore, no advertising of any kind may appear on Bell System vehicles. This applies to Yellow Pages decals and posters."

In closing, remember that modern paints and refinishing techniques should be used. The truck's make and year should be painted on both sides in small, tasteful lettering since most people even faintly interested in old trucks will

To complete the interior restoration, an old registering farebox was found and rebuilt. Advertising car cards, which run along both sides of the ceiling, were obtained from a railroad museum. All work was done in the agency's own shop. *Monterey-Salinas Transit*

Portions of a fleet-painting chart for tank trucks. *The Dawes Arboretum, Newark, Ohio*

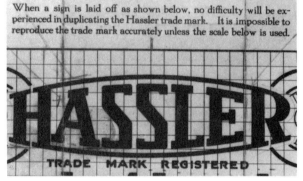

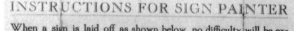

Instructions to a sign painter for arranging lettering for shock absorber trade names to be placed in a "slip-on" body for Ford Model T coupes. *American Truck Historical Society*

make that their logical first question. Also, the style of lettering should be of the same period as when the truck was new. Pictures throughout this book provide ideas.

Some historical research is necessary to discover colors, wording, and lettering styles used by the firm restoring the truck. An article in the June 1987 issue of *The Private Carrier* tells of computer-generated fleet graphics, including reproduced logos. One can perhaps take an old logo and use this method to have it made into a truck decal.

When choosing colors, don't hesitate to be bold. Many old trucks were brightly painted. If you're restoring a truck to be used in a parade, make it stand out in all the color, noise, and excitement associated with the Fourth of July!

Antique Ford Repaint Manual, Authentic Color Chips & Formulas. Nashville, TN: Polyprints, Inc.

Automobile Quarterly Magazine Editors. *General Motors—The First 75 Years of Transportation Products*. Princeton, NJ: Automobile Quarterly Publications, 1983.

Bartlett, John T. "Advertising Aspects of Truck Painting." *The Automobile Trimmer and Painter* (October 1925): 53-54.

Bartlett, John T. "The Possibilities in Colors for Truck Advertising." *The Automobile Trimmer and Painter* (March 1925): 67-68.

Bell System Vehicle Graphics Manual. New York: AT&T, 1975.

Benson, H. L. "The Art of Vehicle Painting." *The Automobile Trimmer and Painter* (March 1926): 42-43.

"Blue Bird Flies into 60th Year." *Wheels of Time* (May/June 1985): 10-12.

"Born Again Labatt's Streamliner." *Wheels of Time* (May/June 1985): 30-31.

Bovee, Cortland L., and William F. Arens. *Contemporary Advertising*, Homewood, IL: Irwin, 1982.

Bradshaw, A. "Good Looks Sell Good Humors." *Commercial Car Journal* (May 1939): 32-33, 99, 103-105.

Burness, Tad. *American Truck & Bus Spotter's Guide—1920-1985*. Osceola, WI: Motorbooks International, 1985.

Burness, Tad. *Pickup and Van Spotter's Guide—1945-1982*. Osceola, WI: Motorbooks International, 1982.

Bush, Donald J. *The Streamlined Decade*. New York: George Braziller, 1975.

Cretors & Co. Catalog, 1913. Reprinted by the Vestal Press, Vestal, NY.

Dahmer, Dick. "Old Trucks in Advertising." *Wheels of Time* (March/April 1991): 34-36.

Eibell, A. F. "How to Do Expert Striping." *The Automobile Trimmer and Painter* (August 1927): 52-53.

"Goodyear's Wingfoot Express…, Milestone in Trucking History." *Wheels of Time* (July/August 1984): 14-16.

Gunnell, John. "Restoring Old Trucks." *Double Clutch* (March/April 1987): 18-22.

Gunnell, John, editor. *Standard Catalog of American Light Duty Trucks*. Iola, WI: Krause Publications, 1987.

Haggard, J.M. "Streamlining of Commercial Bodies and Tanks Keynote in Modern Trend." *The Autobody Trimmer and Painter* (March 1934): 14-15.

Harland, Maurice. "Transfers and Tools." *Signs of the Times* (February 1935): 56-58.

Hils, Mack. *Restoring the Model "A" Pickup*. Moberly, MO: Mack Hils, 1982.

Humphrey, George. "Restoration Tips." *Wheels of Time* (September/October 1983): 10-12.

Keller, Francis J. "Living with It—1947 Ford/Marmon-Herrington." *Special-Interest Autos* (August 1978): 24-27.

"Ken Self, Retired Freightliner Chief Executive, Builds Super 2/3-Scale Model of 1960 Series 31." *Wheels of Time* (July/Augus 1985): 32-34.

Knudson, Leigh. "How to Restore an Old Truck." *Wheels of Time* (May/June 1986): 30-32.

Knudson, Leigh. "Restoring Early Truck Bodies." *Wheels of Time* (March/April 1988): 20-21.

"Let There Be Light on Trucks at Night." *Commercial Car Journal* (October 1934).

MacClary, John Stewart. "Shoe Shop Delivery Truck." *The Automobile Trimmer and Painter* (March 1931): 59-63.

McMillan, A. G. *Ford Model A/AA Truck Owner*. Arcadia, CA: Post-Era Books, 1975.

Meikle, Jeffrey L. *Twentieth Century Limited, Industrial Design in America, 1925-1939*. Philadelphia: Temple Univ. Press, 1979.

Miskella, William J. "Automobile Japanning." *The Automobile Trimmer and Painter* (March 1926): 48-52.

Montville, John B. *Mack*. Newfoundland, NJ: Haessner, 1973.

"Most Beautiful Truck Now Being Exhibited." *Motor Truck & Equipment* (July 1937): 12.

Novins, J. K. "How to Develop Profitable Commercial Business." *The Automobile Trimmer and Painter* (March 1930).

Oakley, Wilbert. "Automobile Finishing: Then and Now." *The Automobile Trimmer and Painter* (July 1930): 52-53.

"Organ-Equipped Truck Ballyhoos Movie." *The Motor Truck* (April 1928): 15.

"'Our Streamlined Vans Bring Business,' says Baillargeon." *Motor Truck & Equipment* (February 1937): 1.

Ousbey, John H. "Coachpainting." *Motor Body* (February 1963): 37-38.

Pardue, Don. "Trucks Carry More Than Freight." *The Private Carrier* (June 1985): 8-13.

Rawson, Bart. "Bennett's Painted Trailer." *Wheels of Time* (March/April 1992): 11.

Rawson, Bart. "Wienermobiles—a 55-year Odyssey." *Wheels of Time* (January/February 1991): 10-11.

Roll, Robert M. *American Trucking: A Seventy-five Year Odyssey*. Osceola, WI: Motorbooks International, 1979.

Reidler, Richard. "Computers Revolutionizing Fleet Graphics." *The Private Carrier* (June 1987): 13-14.

Rose, Floyd A. "How the Body Shop Can Profit with Decalcomania Transfers." *The Automobile Trimmer and Painter* (February 1935): 20-23.

Scroggins, Roy I. "Productmobiles." *Special-Interest Autos* (September/October 1976): 39-43.

Sherwin-Williams. *How Kem Finishes Serve the World's Transportation*. Cleveland, OH: the Company, 1934.

Shondell, W. Joseph. "History of Fleet Graphics." *The Private Carrier* (June 1985): 34, 37.

Simon, Samuel. "Motor-Truck Body Construction." *The Automobile Trimmer and Painter* (January 1930): 41-42.

Sloan, Alfred P., Jr. *My Years With General Motors*. New York, NY: Doubleday, 1963.

Smith, LeRoi. *How to Fix Up Old Cars*. New York: Dodd, Mead & Co., 1968.

Sorensen, Lorin. *The Commercial Fords*. St. Helena, CA: Silverado Publishing Co., 1984.

Staley, Richard A. "Fleet Marking Advantages, Your Trucks Are You . . . Why Not Say So?" *The Private Carrier* (June 1984): 34-36.

Staley, Richard A. *The Visual Impact of Trucks in Traffic*. Washington, DC: American Trucking Associations, 1977.

Stern, Marc. "Moxie's Four-Legged Productmobiles." *Special-Interest Autos* (April 1982): 52-55.

Stitts, E. W. *Stitt's Guidebook for Rejuvenation of Elderly Autos*. 4th ed. Churchtown, PA: E.W. Stitts, 1983.

"Streamlined Commercial Cars." *Autobody Trimmer and Painter* (February 1935): 30.

"Traveling Salesroom." *The Autobody Trimmer and Painter* (April 1931): 39-40.

Wentz, Walt. *Bringing Out the Big Ones—Log Trucking in Oregon, 1912-1983*. Salem, OR: Oregon Forest Products Transportation Association, 1983.

West, Bill. "W. Everett Miller, Designer and Engineer." *Wheels of Time* (March/April 1984): 12-13.

"Wingfoot Express Readied for GAR." *Old Cars Weekly* (February 7, 1985): 1, 9.

Wood, Donald F. "Just One Quart Today, A Short History of Driver/Salesman Trucks." *Special-Interest Autos* (November/December 1975): 39-43.

Wood, Donald F. "The Truck-Borne Advertisements." *Wheels of Time* (February 1981): 8-10.

Wood, Donald F. "Time Out for the Following Commercials." *Special-Interest Autos* (February 1979): 18-25.

Wren, James A., and Genevieve J. Wren. *Motor Trucks of America*. Ann Arbor, MI: University of Michigan Press, 1979.

Old Truck Publications and Organizations

Many publications and organizations can be of assistance to the potential old truck restorer. The few listed here can be used as leads to the others.

Hemmings Motor News is a monthly magazine that contains mostly ads about old autos and trucks for sale and also has ads listing parts, restoration services, literature, and so on. Subscription information can be obtained by writing to: HMN Subscriptions, Box 100, Bennington, VT 05201. Hemmings also occasionally publishes the *Hemmings Vintage Auto Almanac,* which is a large directory of firms and groups interested in old car and truck restoration.

Old Cars Weekly is a newspaper with both stories and ads of interest to old car and truck fans. Subscription information is available from Old Cars Weekly, 700 E. State St., Iola, WI 54990.

Classic Motorbooks (P. O. Box 1, Osceola, WI 54020) probably has the largest assortment of books for sale dealing with auto and truck restoration.

The American Truck Historical Society (P. O. Box 531168, Birmingham, AL 35253) is the largest, most active group interested in the history of trucks and trucking. It publishes a magazine, *Wheels of Time,* and has over fifty local chapters throughout the country and in Canada. It also offers specialized advice and help in the restoration of trucks.

The Light Commercial Vehicle Association can be reached c/o Tom Brownell, P. O. Box 1162, Big Rapids, MI 49307. This group is interested in smaller trucks (possibly up to 1 1/2 tons). It publishes a helpful newsletter, *This Old Truck,* and lists technical advisors for most makes of light trucks.

The Antique Truck Club of America, whose membership appears concentrated in the Northeast, publishes a magazine, *Double Clutch.* Its address is P. O. Box 291, Hershey, PA 17033.

Any of these sources is recommended for the individual interested in learning more about truck history and restoration. There are also groups interested in special body applications, such as tow trucks, military, and fire-fighting. There are many smaller, more specialized groups ("networks" might be a better term) of individuals who help each other out. In any event, the person or firm contemplating restoring and using an old truck for advertising would benefit much from looking into any of the abovementioned groups.

Index